# RAVENS unseen evil unwilling eyes

## Paul L. Cox
### with Jerry Seiden

Apple Valley, CA

Copyright 2000 by Aslan's Place
*All Rights Reserved.*

No part of this publication may be reproduced, stored in a retrieval system, or transmitted in any form or by any means—electronic, mechanical, photocopy, recording, or any other—except for brief quotations embodied in critical articles or printed reviews, without prior permission of the publisher.

Scripture taken from the HOLY BIBLE, NEW INTERNATIONAL VERSION. Copyright © 1973, 1978, 1984 International Bible Society. Used by permission of Zondervan Bible Publishers.

Cover and book design by Chad M. Upham

ISBN 0-9702138-0-3

Published by
Aslan's Place
P.O. Box 3902
Apple Valley, CA 92307
www.aslansplace.com

RECOMMENDED BY CHRISTIAN LEADERS

"This book is a treasure of rich experiences. With writing that is both pleasant to read and gripping, Dr. Paul Cox describes for us the spiritual conflict—the battle that is waged silently by millions of people that cry out for freedom in Jesus. Behind that which is obvious there exists a spiritual reality. The ministry of Dr. Paul Cox will put salve on your eyes to help you discover the real reason for so much pain, and the authority we have in Christ."

**Rev. Claudio Freidzon**
**Rey de Reyes Iglesia,**
**Buenos Aires, Argentina**

"Helpful reading for anyone who is preparing for Christian ministry with practical illustrations. You'll relate. This book will provide a clearer understanding of spiritual warfare and the attachment of demons and how Christ's victory brings deliverance for the believer."

**David and Bonnie Juroe**
**Ministers and therapists**

"I know the Paul Cox produced by the lessons of *Ravens*. The ministry that God has brought forth in and from this man have impacted me, my family and our congregation at a deep level. What you read here has come out of the fire. As you read, I pray that the fire of God will touch you as it has Paul Cox."

**Rev. Rich Marshall**
**ROI Ministry**

"Dr. Cox captures the tension between the sovereignty of God and the choices we have to make. God sovereignly sought him out for this ministry. God sovereignly allowed children to suffer demonic assault through no fault of their own. But eventually it always came back to people's choices to obey God or resist the work of the Spirit."

**Rev. Arthur Burk**
**Plumbline Ministries**

## RECOMMENDED BY CHRISTIAN LEADERS

"We highly recommend this book to anyone who has a spiritual hunger to see God's reality unfold more in his daily life. Paul is a dear friend to us from whom we have learned a lot. His sincerity and humility build a solid foundation for his outstanding gift of discernment. When you read this book keep your spiritual eyes open and begin to discern more of your own spiritual environment. You too are not fighting against flesh and blood, but against spiritual beings. Whatever situation you are in right now, there is hope for you and your house. This book could be a key for you to succeed."

**Axel & Angelika Jagemann**
**Leaders of Hope for Munich**
**Munich, Germany**

"If you are looking for a textbook on deliverance, this is it! Paul Cox has given us a very personal look into his journey from tradition to deliverance. *Ravens* is a practical book that will benefit all who read it, and especially those desiring to be set free."

**Gary and Carolyn Abke**
**Directors of Senior Adult Ministries**
**The Church on the Way**

# Dedication

THIS BOOK IS DEDICATED TO MY FAMILY: my wife Donna of over 30 years, and my three children, Brian, Christy, and Corrie. Thank you for your patience with me as I moved into a new understanding of the power of God.

This book is also dedicated to all the intercessors who prayed me into a deeper relationship with our Lord. I especially thank Mae Young, Linda Fimbres, Bonnie Jones, Jackie Douglas-Thomas, and Brian and Terry Lynn Fairley.

# Foreword

THIS BOOK IS A COMMON STORY to many of us in ministry. It is the collective experience of a number of individuals. The story is a chronicle of the call that God places on certain men and women in Christian service. It is not a call to ministry—that happens years before. Rather, this is a call to battle.

To those of us who have walked this path, the story is personal—often painful. We bear the scars of conflict—scars inflicted by the flock. Still, no person in ministry would expose or embarrass a member of the flock. For that reason, this work takes the form of fiction. Any resemblance to specific individuals, living or dead, is purely coincidental. The truth of this experience lies in the principles, not the personalities, in the story.

The coming of the Spirit was gradual in our lives and work. However, we are tempted to impart all that we know—immediately—to any willing listener. But we know better than to do that. In fact, we tell new leaders not to dispense information that people won't know how to use.

This work is a primer, an introduction to spiritual conflict. It is a vehicle to communicate the early lessons and experiences that await anyone who has a calling similar to ours. May God use it to shape their understanding, prepare them for ministry, and confirm their experience.

We have already prayed for you, the reader. Before you purchased this book or read these words, we asked God to send a blessing to you. Receive it now.

# Chapter 1

It was a secret. A dark secret. A shameful secret that was hidden from us all. *Who would have believed it? I wondered. Still, I should have seen the signs, the struggles. Why didn't I notice his need?*

It had been twenty-seven years. Richard was now a man, and he had a wife and one child. But I could still see in him the young boy that I knew—or thought I knew.

"Hi, Pastor Greg. I heard you were in town. That was a good sermon tonight. I didn't know you could preach to adults." Richard's face was straight, and his eyes were glassy. His gaze passed through me.

"Well, after I grew up, I got a chance to see the real world. They let me out of our small town and couldn't get me back in there. What about you, Richard? I heard you were in the hospital."

"I got out today," he answered. "But I'm not sick. I'm crazy."

"I don't believe that," I shot back without thought.

"It's what they say," Richard answered. "I can't handle life—never could."

"Of all my friends, you had a special spark. Girls hung around you like bees to clover. Other kids looked to you and followed your lead. I just knew you'd be in ministry."

"I was a good actor. 'Image is everything,' my dad used to tell me. You know what else my dad told me?" Richard searched for my eyes. He seemed to thaw a bit. "My dad said, 'At least pretend like you've got a brain, Richard. Don't embarrass me at church. I can't image how you could be my son!'"

"I'm sorry, Richard. I didn't know. I thought your dad was—"

Richard interrupted, "You thought my dad was a great guy. Everybody did. I did, too. I even believed he was right about me. He said I'd never amount to anything."

I reached out my hand and touched Richard's arm. I wanted to offer a little comfort, but he pulled away. His eyes were fixed on my hand. He watched for any movement and said, "My dad only touched me when he needed to teach me a lesson. I never learned anything though—except that I didn't like the lesson."

"Are you ready to go, Greg," my host called out and motioned for me to follow.

"You better go," Richard said. "I won't waste any more of your time."

"Richard, you didn't waste my time. I wanted to talk to you. I'd like to talk again. Can we?"

Without a word, Richard wrote down his number and handed it to me. "You can call me. I'll understand if you don't." He turned to leave but stopped short. "Oh, Pastor Greg, I almost forgot why I came to talk to you. I wanted to tell you something."

# CHAPTER 1

"What is it, Richard?"

"On each side of you there are warriors. All the time you spoke I saw them."

"Warriors?" I asked.

"God's protection," he answered. "Maybe you don't see them, but you need them." Richard turned away but continued to speak, "Maybe there's a lot you don't see. And didn't see."

I didn't have time to respond. My host pulled me by the elbow, and Richard found his exit.

"Don't mind him, Greg," my host said. "He's probably loaded up on half-a-dozen medications. His head is full of hallucinations. Don't give it a thought."

"How does that happen?" I asked my host, the pastor of the church. We were in the car and headed to some coffee shop. I should have been ready for pie and hot tea. Instead, I was puzzled and confused.

"What? You're not still thinkin' about what's-his-name?"

"Richard. Yeah, I'm thinking of Richard."

"I told ya, Greg, that man has a head full of fantasies, and he's full of drugs, too. That's the way they treat guys like him these days. They figure as long as they're sedated and settled down, they won't cause trouble."

"No," I insisted, "Richard is different. All through high school he stood out. God had His hand on him. This isn't right. Something or somebody stopped him. I need to call him."

"What? Now?"

"No. Right now I need some pie and hot tea with an old friend."

# Chapter 2

"Hello, Richard?"

"Yeah. I knew you'd call today," Richard answered, his voice still limp.

"Well, I wanted to—uh—that is to say, I felt like I was supposed to . . . well, call you and . . . uh—"

"Offer me some help?" Richard added.

"Right. That's it. I thought there might be something I could do to help."

"Pastor Greg, can I ask you a question?"

"Sure, anything."

"Well," Richard continued, "when the great Old Testament prophet Elijah needed to be hidden and fed, God told him to go to the brook Cherith. Do you remember how God fed him there?"

"Ravens. God sent Ravens to feed him," I answered.

"And then later, a poor widow." Richard paused and breathed a big sigh. "I wonder if Elijah complained about the provisions and the way he was served. Or did he just take what the ravens brought? Did he remember that it came from God?"

## CHAPTER 2

I didn't know if the questions were rhetorical, but I filled in the silence. "I'll bet he was glad to get the food however it came."

"Pastor Greg, do you think it's possible that maybe you're not supposed to help *me*. Maybe, instead, God wants me to help *you*?"

"Well . . . uh . . . Richard, I've always known that God had His hand on you. I'm sure He could use you to teach me. But right now, I'm just so full of questions—concern about you. Maybe we could meet and maybe you could help me understand what happened in your life to . . . well . . . I mean—"

"To make me crack?"

"No. I care about you, Richard. I even feel responsible in some ways."

"Don't, Greg. You didn't make my childhood miserable—my mother did. You didn't tell me that I was the rot that infected my family—my father did. But even they weren't the reasons. They didn't dig the pits into which I fell. Someone else lay behind it."

"What do you mean, Richard? Who?"

"The one who moved Joseph's brothers to sell him into slavery. The one who led Pharaoh to toss the baby boys into the Nile. The one who pushed Saul to throw spears at David. The one who enraged Herod to slaughter in Bethlehem. The one who tempted Judas with thirty pieces of silver. The one who wants to stop you, Greg. He digs the pits. He builds the prisons. But God wants to give you the ladders and the keys. Are you hungry, Pastor Greg? Are you afraid of ravens?"

# Chapter 3

"You didn't have to buy me lunch," Richard said. His eyes fixed on the menu. "We could have talked anywhere. I don't mind."

"I wanted to fellowship with you, Richard. And food has a way of making things seem—"

"Less formal?" Richard inserted.

"No. I was about to say 'more friendly.' Plus, I love the chips and salsa at this place. It's hard for anyone to be sophisticated or stuffy while crunching chips and begging the waiter for more water."

"We don't eat out much anymore," Richard said. He held a chip, examined each side, and then set it by his water glass. "I am on a leave of absence from my position as a youth pastor."

"Leave of absence?"

"Yeah. I'm not working now. The official reason for the leave of absence is PTS. Do you know what that is, Pastor Greg?"

"Post-traumatic stress. Isn't that something veterans get? I mean, isn't it a result of war?"

"War, huh?!" Richard launched the words, a breathy scoff like an inside joke that only he understood. Then he lifted his head like a periscope and turned in his seat to spy the restaurant and its patrons. "My kid would like this place. I'll have to bring him here when things are better. They will get better, won't they, Pastor Greg?"

"I know that my Redeemer lives, and that in the end He will stand upon the earth. And after my skin has been destroyed, yet in my flesh I will see God; I myself will see him with my own eyes— I, and not another. How my heart yearns within me!"

"Job 19. Funny that you would quote Job to me."

"Why's it funny, Richard?"

"Because I've lived in Job for the past months. I went there looking for comfort."

"Did you find it?" I asked.

Richard didn't answer right away. He looked me squarely in the eyes. It was the first time that he had really connected and reached out to me. His eyes held mine, and his spirit cried out. I could hear the groan and the hunger of his heart. He wondered if I was safe, if I was someone he could trust. But there was more. I thought that he wanted a like-minded spirit, a brother to share his journey, someone who would understand. *If only I knew your path*, I thought. *Poor Richard, you seem so lost.*

"I found more than comfort in Job. I found the God of all comfort. I found my source and my supply. My provider and my protector. My focus and my faith. My king and my kindred redeemer.

"Do you know what, Pastor Greg? Like Job, I needed to be stripped naked of all rights and reputation. Every comforter needed to fail. Every argument needed to cease. In my pit and in my pity, I had nowhere to look—except up. In the glare of the sunlight,

I saw a hand reach down for me."

Richard's eyes released streams of tears down each cheek. He swallowed hard and spoke through the emotion. "It was the hand of God. He lifted me out. He gave me my mind and my mission. And He told me that you would come."

"I'll do what I can to help, Richard, but—"

"This isn't about me. God has more in mind than help for me. God brought us together for *His* purpose. You've been drafted, Pastor Greg. Remember when I told you that I saw two warriors on each side of you as you spoke?"

"Sure, Richard. But I understand. You were tired—it was late. And you had just gotten—"

"Greg, I wasn't delusional. I was delighted—though it was hard to show. I saw more than just two warriors, but I couldn't tell you then. I saw three at the pulpit. And the hand of God rested like a cloak upon the third, the one in the middle."

# Chapter 4

"Pastor Greg, it's your favorite board member on line two. He wants to know if you're in the office today. What should I say?"

"Thanks, Sandy. I'll take it." I took a deep breath and then picked up the phone. "Good morning, Fred."

"I had a hunch you'd be in the office today. Isn't it your day off? Or did you make another change and forget to tell your board?"

"No, you're right. It's my day off." It was a struggle to speak to Fred. I didn't want polite conversation. I didn't want any conversation with him. "So, what's up? What I can I do for you?"

"Do I have to have a reason to call my pastor? Maybe I just wanted to chat."

"Okay, a chat about what?"

"Now see, Greg. There it is. You're so serious, so bottom-line—all business. That's why people don't seem to connect with you."

I could feel a surge in my chest. I wanted to strike out, but I didn't know how. Whatever I said would be wrong. Fred could twist any comment into a weapon. I knew I'd better ignore his comment and just try to end the call. I said, "Listen, Fred, I just came in to

## CHAPTER 4

pick up a few books for Sunday's sermon. I told Martha that I'd be at home today."

"By the way, Greg, that sermon on Sunday was something else. I can sure tell when you've had time to study."

"Or when I haven't?" I shot back.

"Now, don't be hard on yourself, Greg. Take a little pleasure in those times when you get it right. Like this last Sunday. Why, I'd say that your sermon was a number . . . well . . . let's just say you rang the bell, Greg. Now, I'd better let you get home to that lovely wife. You'll tell Martha that I said 'hello,' won't you?"

"Sure, Fred. Whatever you say."

"Oh, and Greg. You won't take too many books home will you? God knows, you need a little rest. Bye now."

# Chapter 5

"That smells good, Greg. What are you cookin'?" Martha was home. She followed her nose to find me. I didn't answer fast enough. She lifted the lids, looked in each pot, surveyed the kitchen for damage, and added, "Or maybe I should ask *why* you are cooking?"

"I made Swiss steak. I went to the store and got the toughest meat I could find. Then I took that meat hammer of yours, and I beat it. I beat it until I figured it knew who was boss."

Martha lifted the lid again, spied the meat, and said, "You're supposed to tenderize not terrorize." She put her purse on the counter and joined me at the table. "You probably didn't even need to pressure cook it."

"Oh, no. I pressure cooked it. I wasn't gonna let it get off that easy."

"And it looks like you mashed the potatoes and creamed the corn, too. I see a real theme in tonight's dinner. Mind telling me what inspired this show of food and force?"

"Let me ask you something, Martha. Everybody knows that today is my day off, right? I mean—it's been my day off for years.

It's even in the bulletin and on the calendar." Martha listened but started to set the table. "Well, then, why would he call my office just to talk? There was no emergency, no pressing concern—just a phone call to ruin my day off."

"Well, I hope he calls every week if it means you'll make dinner." I wasn't amused. So Martha stopped her preparations, sat back down, and asked, "But who is *he*?"

"Fred."

"Oh, I see."

We sat in silence for a moment. Martha broke the quiet and said, "Well, if Fred was aiming to ruin your day, I'd say he got his way."

"That's what bugs me. I let folks like Fred have power over me. Like when I'm preaching. I see 'em out there and next thing I know, I try to avoid even looking to that part of the sanctuary. Wherever people like him are seated, I feel a cold and dark spot. They're wet blankets. No, it's worse—when I look at or reach out to them, I get back a feeling I can't explain."

"What do you mean you 'get back'?"

"Well, preaching is like radar or sonar. It's not just a blind transmission. With every point and word of proclamation, people reflect back a sort of response. Most folk—unless they're asleep—send back a warm echo and a spiritual signal that connects with me. I know it sounds crazy. But folks like Fred, and the satellites that spin around him, don't connect—not with me anyway. They don't even seem to hear me. It's like I'm speaking another language."

## CHAPTER 5

"Well, my stomach is speaking another language, but I know what it means," Martha said. "Let's just pray that God tenderizes old Fred half as well as you did this meat."

# Chapter 6

"Are you sure you wouldn't rather talk in my office?"

"No, Pastor Greg. I want to be here in the sanctuary," answered Richard. He turned slowly and took in every aspect of the worship center. "I want every word we speak and every prayer we pray to be heard."

"I can hear just fine in my office."

"I know, but I don't mean you." Richard stood, stepped up on the platform, peered into the baptismal, and circled the pulpit. Then he came back to me and settled in the empty pew just ahead. For a long while, he sat silent. His only sounds were an occasional grunt or moan, like he had insight or indigestion.

I got curious, and a little impatient. I asked, "Well, Richard, what do you think? Would you like to pray or talk?"

Richard turned. His intensity was almost scary. "Pastor Greg, do you think this thing with Fred and others like him is a personality conflict? Do you see it as a clash of vision or purpose? Or maybe a power struggle between well-meaning church folk?"

## CHAPTER 6

"I don't know. I've been in ministry for years. I've seen lots of this stuff. And after almost nine years here, maybe it's time...."

Richard wouldn't let me finish. He interrupted, "Time to leave? Leave now? When you are most experienced and best equipped to pastor this place? It takes a pastor three years just to get settled in a church. The community needs four or five. Yet most pastors don't even stay two years. You've beaten the odds and stayed. You know too much. That means you're dangerous, and they don't want you here."

I wanted to reach out to Richard and settle him, but I remembered the last time I had touched him. Instead, I asked, "Are you okay? I mean, have you been taking the medication and following doctor's orders?"

"You don't get it, do you?"

"I'm not sure I understand what you're driving at, Richard—if that's what you mean. But I care about you, and I want to help."

He pointed to the pew pocket. It held hymnals, Bibles, response cards, and a left-over bulletin covered with childish scribbles. "Pick up the Bible. Turn to Ephesians 6." I hesitated. I don't like to be patronized or pushed. Richard saw the rub. He softened, held my eyes, and whispered, "Please?"

I reached for the pew Bible and found Ephesians 6. Richard said, "Start reading at verse 10. But first, before you read, do you remember what I said when you first expressed concern for me? You said you felt a little responsible. Do you remember what I said about my parents? I told you that even they weren't the real problem. Someone else lay behind it all."

## CHAPTER 6

"Sure. I remember."

"The same is true for you, Pastor Greg, and this place." Richard swept his arm and gaze through the sanctuary and the air above him. "Fred and those with him and those who will come after him are only tools in the hands of others. It is the force behind them that should concern you. They are at work to move you on or bury you under."

"Now, Richard, don't you think—"

"Please, Pastor Greg, just read. And read it like it was written for you."

"Alright...

> Finally, be strong in the Lord and in his mighty power. Put on the full armor of God so that you can take your stand against the devil's schemes. For our struggle is not against flesh and blood, but against the rulers, against the authorities, against the powers of this dark world and against the spiritual forces of evil in the heavenly realms.
>
> Therefore put on the full armor of God, so that when the day of evil comes, you may be able to stand your ground, and after you have done everything, to stand. Stand firm then, with the belt of truth buckled around your waist, with the breastplate of righteousness in place, and with your feet fitted with the readiness that comes from the gospel of peace. In addition to all this, take up the shield of faith, with which you can extinguish all the flaming arrows of the evil one. Take the helmet of salvation and the sword of the Spirit, which is the word of God.
>
> And pray in the Spirit on all occasions with all kinds of prayers and requests. With this in mind, be alert and always keep on praying for all the saints. Pray also for me, that whenever I open my mouth, words may be given me so that I will fearlessly make known the mystery of the gospel, for which I am an ambassador in chains. Pray that I may declare it fearlessly, as I should.

## CHAPTER 6

"Pastor Greg, it sounds like the apostle Paul knew that the forces of darkness did not want him to open his mouth. He knew that this battle was real, and he enlisted others to pray, prepare, and protect themselves. Do you believe this?"

"Of course I do. You know I do. We talked about this when we were in high school together."

"Right, I remember—along with all the other youth who heard our high school sponsor speak. He told us that the devil wanted us to smoke, drink, use drugs, and have sex. He told us to be good kids, resist the devil, and avoid all those vices. But there's more to it than that. The devil's aim is higher. The devil didn't tempt the apostle Paul with cigarettes. He tried to keep Paul from cities. The apostle reached for the keys to unlock kingdoms and nations. Wherever Paul tread, he established the rulership of Christ. He brought God's kingdom to thousands—and, in time, millions—of people."

"Paul was dangerous to the powers of darkness, to the rulers of this world. They met him at every turn and fought his every advance. Yet, with prayer, Paul saw God frustrate the plans and power of the enemy. What Satan intended for harm, God turned to good. Even Paul's imprisonments became platforms for preaching—all the way to Caesar's court."

"Richard, I believe the Bible, and I understand this text. But I'm no apostle Paul. I'm small potatoes. The devil isn't losing sleep over me."

Just then, a rush of air filled the sanctuary. The back doors swung open and a loud voice called, "Well, fancy this! The secretary told me that I'd find my pastor in the sanctuary. I was afraid you might be on your knees. Of course, I couldn't interrupt you then, could I?"

"What can I do for you, Fred?"

# Chapter 7

I STOOD TO MEET FRED AT THE SANCTUARY DOORS. Richard moved toward the front to pray. I took Fred's hand and greeted him. Richard knelt on the steps below the pulpit. Fred said, "I don't mean to bother you, Greg, but...." He couldn't finish his thought. Richard prayed out loud and distracted him.

Richard had opened the Bible. He read and prayed Psalm 2:

> *Why do the heathen rage,*
> *and the people imagine a vain thing?*
> *The kings of the earth set themselves,*
> *and the rulers take counsel together,*
> *against the Lord, and against his anointed, saying,*
> *Let us break their bands asunder,*
> *and cast away their cords from us.*
> *He that sitteth in the heavens shall laugh:*
> *the Lord shall have them in derision.*
> *Then shall he speak unto them in his wrath,*
> *and vex them in his sore displeasure.*

"A very troubled man," Fred said with a nod toward Richard.

"Why do you say that?" I asked.

"Well, what sort of nonsense is he babbling?"

"He's reading the Psalms, Fred. Listen."

# CHAPTER 7

Richard lifted his voice as if he read to a crowd. I could see the preacher in him—the minister I'd recognized years before. He proclaimed each verse like it was his own:

> Yet have I set my king upon my holy hill of Zion.
> I will declare the decree: the Lord hath said unto me,
> Thou art my Son; this day have I begotten thee.
> Ask of me, and I shall give thee the heathen for thine inheritance,
> and the uttermost parts of the earth for thy possession.
> Thou shalt break them with a rod of iron;
> thou shalt dash them in pieces like a potter's vessel.
> Be wise now therefore, O ye kings:
> be instructed, ye judges of the earth.
> Serve the Lord with fear,
> and rejoice with trembling.
> Kiss the Son, lest he be angry, and ye perish from the way,
> when his wrath is kindled but a little.
> Blessed are all they that put their trust in him.

I turned to Fred, but he was gone. The doors swung a bit till they found their center mark and stood still. It was as if Fred hadn't been there. And I felt called into the atmosphere that Richard had created or invited.

The Bible lay open on the step, and Richard stood tall upon the platform. Like a tree in a strong wind, he swayed back and forth in rhythm with the song he sang. His arms and hands and movement seem to sweep the sanctuary clean. The gray cloud that filled that place was gone. The weight that pulled me down, burdened my spirit, and tied my tongue was lifted. I wanted to enter into whatever Richard had opened, but I didn't know how. It didn't matter; it was enough just to eat the crumbs that fell.

# Chapter 8

THE PHONE RANG SEVERAL TIMES. I was tempted to hang up. *It's too early*, I thought. *You'll disturb the whole family*. Still, I couldn't hang up. I was unsettled inside, and I sensed that Richard could help. I let it ring two more times, and Richard answered.

"I'm sorry to bother you so early, Richard."

"No bother. The wife and the kids are already gone. I was just having my quiet time. And I was thinking about you, too."

"Well, I feel a little awkward saying this, but ... uhm ... I guess ... well. It's just that I feel a kind of connectedness with you. It's like you have something for me."

"And you for me," Richard added. "It's not good for man to be alone, you know. And I think God meant more than marriage. Moses had his Aaron. Jonathan had his armorbearer. Paul had Silas and Luke. Jesus had Peter, James, and John."

"I'm glad you said that. I'm not sure who else I can talk to about some of these things."

"Things?" Richard asked.

"Like last night. I had a dream. It still troubles me. I'm not the kind of guy who gets a lot of dreams—significant dreams, anyway. But it's like a part of me got switched on."

"Maybe you ought to do what Eli told Samuel."

"What do you mean?"

"Samuel, the Old Testament prophet and priest was a young boy when he began ministry in God's tabernacle. And God communicated an important message through him. It was a tough and dry time in Israel then, spiritually speaking. There were no visions, and the Bible says that the word of the Lord was rare in those day. Still, God spoke to the boy. He spoke to Samuel, but Samuel didn't understand that it was God's voice. So Eli, the old and blind prophet and priest told the boy, 'Go, lie down: and it shall be, if he call thee, that thou shalt say, Speak, LORD; for thy servant heareth.'

"The God who made our mouths certainly can speak for Himself. We just need to tell Him that we're listening." Then Richard paused for a moment and said, "So, I'm listening, too. What was your dream?"

"It was probably the pizza," I scoffed. "But maybe it will mean something to you. In the dream, I was a sort of witness to an attack. A man cried out. He wanted help, but I couldn't see the problem. I dared to go closer, and then I saw what it was."

"Snakes," Richard said.

"Yes! How did you know?"

"Maybe I had the same pizza. Please continue."

"It was a dry desert wash. I walked through tumbleweeds and brush. Snakes flew up and attacked. Without fear, I swatted them

## CHAPTER 8

like flies and continued to walk."

"The man called out to you. He pleaded for you to help. He had no power over the snakes. They attacked and bit him. One would drop and another would lunge. Each one drove fangs and shot venom into the man. The sight sickened you. His flesh was swollen. His face was deformed. But you pressed on, and you defended him and saved him. The man called you by name, but you didn't know his name—my name."

I hung up the phone.

The phone rang. I didn't want to touch it. I wiped my sweaty palms on my shirt. I knew it was Richard. I let it ring. *This isn't right*, I thought. *Things like this don't happen. Not to me, anyway. I don't need this.* Still, I picked up the phone.

"Hello?"

"Why did you hang up?" Richard asked.

"Why don't *you* tell me? You seem to know everything."

"Greg, I only know what God reveals. None of this is my idea."

"Richard, how is this possible? How could you know my dream?"

"Because it was *my* dream, too. Remember—Joseph knew Pharaoh's dream because it was his life too. He would live the years of plenty and famine along with Egypt. Joseph knew the baker's dream. He, too, would be called upon to keep Pharaoh's bread basket full. No careless loss would be tolerated. It was Joseph's warning. And Joseph knew the cupbearer's dream. It would lead to Joseph's freedom and joy. It was his dream, too. Soon he would serve the Pharaoh."

## CHAPTER 8

I hung up the phone again.

It rang. *God, I feel childish,* I prayed. *I don't remember ever hanging up on anyone—except maybe you, God.*

It rang on. *God, I can't pick it up now. I'm embarrassed.*

It didn't matter. I had to pick it up. I've been blessed with a streak of responsibility. "Hello?"

"Why did you hang up, Greg?" Richard asked like a child. He didn't understand.

"Because you made too much sense!" I barked. "I know you're right. And being fed by ravens is beginning to test my pride."

"Oh." Richard paused and processed my honesty. "Well, I want you to remember that God's will is no mystery, Pastor Greg. Only those under judgment hear a strange tongue. But God wants His children to know His will. What does Amos say in chapter three? *Surely the Sovereign* LORD *does nothing without revealing his plan to his servants the prophets.* God knows you need a little convincing. This is just His way. So what do you say?"

"I'm not sure. I don't know enough to even answer you."

"That's okay," Richard reassured. "Can I ask you a favor?"

"Sure, of course."

"I want to finish what we started the other day at church. If you'll join me, I'd like to walk around the church and pray tonight."

"Sort of a Jericho march?" I asked.

"Yeah—" Richard hesitated then said, "but kinda the opposite—like Nehemiah's night walk. We don't want to tear this wall down. Somebody has already been doing that. We want to fix the holes and keep out the rats."

# Chapter 9

"Oh, Pastor Greg, you frightened me!" Diana fumbled with her keys and purse. "I was just about to lock up."

"That's okay. We'll be here for a while."

"Maybe all night," Richard said. His eyes were glued to Diana.

"Have we met?" Diana directed the question at Richard then looked to me.

"Oh, jeepers, I'm sorry," I gushed. "Diana, this is my friend Richard Anderson. He has been a friend of mine since we were in high school. He is now on a leave of absence from his position as youth pastor at Agape Christian Fellowship. And Richard this is Diana Nickels. She is our minister of music and a member of our church staff. Diana is a hard worker, and a real perfectionist when it comes to music. Thanks to her, Christmas and Easter are never dull. She cooks up some fantastic productions."

Diana bowed and tilted her head. She put on her evangelist's grin. The crows feet at the corner of her eyes deepened. She purred a bit, then said, "Well, I do try to give the Lord my best."

# CHAPTER 9

Richard had yet to take his eyes off Diana. I'm not sure that he even blinked. I was afraid that Diana would find it uncomfortable. But I was even more afraid of what Richard was about to say. Then he spoke.

"Do you lead worship, or do you direct the music and singing?" Richard asked. It was more quiz than question.

I cleared my throat and played with my keys. But Diana lifted her head, looked to me, and formed her response. Her smile fell and her face flattened. Her eyes were stirred, but her jaw was set—ready for the challenge. She turned in one sharp movement and said, "Well, my job description isn't important. I'm sure you and Pastor Greg have more pressing matters. You are—no doubt—troubled. Why else would you call the pastor out at this late hour? I'll leave you alone. Good night." With that she marched through the foyer and out the door.

Richard's eyes remained on the door. After a long pause, he let out a grunt—maybe it was a groan. He didn't share his thoughts.

I couldn't help but ask, "Richard, you had an intense gaze at Diana. Weren't you afraid that it would make her uncomfortable?"

"No. I wasn't focused on Diana. Anyway, she was already uncomfortable. My eyes were on the reasons why."

# Chapter 10

RICHARD NODDED TOWARD THE SANCTUARY AND SAID, "Let's start in here. Let's just tell the Lord that we are here and ready to do what He has asked."

"And what—exactly—has he asked us to do?" I ventured.

Richard opened his Bible. It was worn and marked. Colored highlighters had illuminated the pages, and notes filled the margins. Richard turned to Ezekiel 22, and he read verses 29 and 30:

> The people of the land practice extortion and commit robbery; they oppress the poor and needy and mistreat the alien, denying them justice. I looked for a man among them who would build up the wall and stand before me in the gap on behalf of the land so I would not have to destroy it, but I found none.

"Pastor Greg, if you knew that someone in your church—or in the community around the church—was being abused or tortured, could you ignore their cries? Would you help them if you could?"

"Well, yes, of course. You know I would. What's your point, Richard?"

"What if they were being robbed or oppressed by bullies? Could you pretend not to hear?"

"I would do what I could. Who do you mean?"

"When Israel suffered in Egyptian bondage, God heard their groans, and he took action. God prepared Moses. He opened his eyes, his ears, and his heart. God equipped Moses to face the enemy and free the people. God is preparing you, too, Pastor Greg. The first lessons are the most painful because He opens your ears and enlightens your eyes. You will hear the groans and see the suffering of your brothers and sisters. The enemy's deeds will be uncovered. The darkness will not be dark to you. You will lose both your ignorance and your innocence." Richard paused, but I knew it was for my sake.

"When you hear the cries, the groans, resist the urge to kill the Egyptian and fight the battle on your own. The Scripture says, *Be strong in the Lord and in his mighty power.* The battle is the Lord's. And our best place is near Him."

Richard turned toward the platform and began to call upon the Lord. I was afraid that God might strike him dead. His prayer was unlike any I've heard. He wasn't disrespectful; he was desperate. He pleaded with God to keep His promises and to honor His own Word. And then he turned to me. Without a break or pause or breath, he placed his hands upon my ears and then his palms over my eyes.

"Oh, Lord, open these ears," he cried. "Take the scales from these eyes. Let your servant see as you see and hear as you hear. Expose the deeds of darkness. Equip him for the fight."

A stillness and quiet settled over Richard. His eyes were closed. The only sound he made was a grunt or a groan, and he occasionally nodded. He listened to a voice that I had yet to hear. He received instructions from an inner source.

Then a change occurred. Richard snapped to attention like a soldier with new orders. He lifted his head and voice. "Greg, I believe the Lord wants me to tell you these words: 'I have come to you this night. Look in your hand—behold the sword of the Lord. Look in your heart—the compassion and justice of God. Look in your mouth—my words flow forth. Look around you—the Lord himself is a wall of protection. None will harm you. They will tear at you and tire you, but you will prevail and do the work to which I have called you.'"

Richard released his hands from my head, but a feeling remained. I was electric. Every part of my body surged with an energy. Then a thought came to me, *This is stupid, Greg. You have given in to the delusions of a crazy man. You are as crazy as he is. What gives him the right to speak for God? Richard is the only thing out of place in this church. Be polite but firm, and send him away.*

Richard's eyes were on me. I was about to express my doubts or mimic the thought, but he spoke first. "I think it was Watchman Nee who said, 'If the Holy Spirit were taken from the earth, most churches would go on business-as-usual.' I don't know where your reliance and strength has been in the past. Maybe you trusted in your education or skill or maybe church programs or curriculum. But from this day on, God wants you to trust in His presence and power. He wants you to be like Moses, who said, *If your Presence does not go with us, do not send us up from here.*"

"Richard, I appreciate your prayers, and I value your zeal. I know you mean well, but remember, I'm not a newcomer to the things of God."

"I know," Richard answered. "If it were just me and my thoughts, I wouldn't open my mouth. I'm just a raven bringing crumbs to the man of God. I don't mind if you discount me. I'm a crazy and depressed nobody with nothing to prove. But—" Richard paused. He cast his eyes to a far corner of the sanctuary. He breathed deeply and then turned back and found my eyes. "But the One calling you is another story. He won't give up. Open up to Him, and let Him prove Himself. He will teach you if you will listen. Let this be the sign, Pastor Greg—your ears will be opened to cries. You will be moved as God is moved. The groans and pleas of those oppressed will be your call to action. If you hear none of this, then I am, indeed, a crazed fool. I will crawl back under my rock, return to my shackles, and remain among the tombs."

"Well, Richard—" I paused to clear my throat and find a response. The moment was pregnant, but I was not about to give birth to anything I couldn't understand or name. Besides, I didn't own any of this. It was all Richard's. I continued, "Listen, I think I'm gonna call it a night. You can work on me some more tomorrow."

"That's okay," Richard said. "We've done what we needed to do." He stood and added, "But I won't *work* on you anymore. It's someone else's job now. Heed His lessons, please. I need you. Remember the dream we shared? When you awoke, the dream and the cries were gone. For me, they are not. Awake or asleep, there is no difference—I live the nightmare."

# Chapter 11

"Hello? Where are you hiding, Greg?"

I poked my head above the pew where I knelt. Fred marched down the center aisle. "My heavens, Pastor! I believe you're spending more time in this sanctuary than in your office. What's the attraction to this place?"

"Well, I think Jesus said that God's house is a house of prayer."

"Greg, what's wrong?" Fred landed in the pew behind me and leaned over to examine my eyes. "Have you been crying? Is there anything I should know? I mean, is there anything I can do?"

"No. These are good tears. God's just plowed up my heart a bit."

"Greg, I've always appreciated your level temperament. I mean, you don't take the congregation on emotional roller-coasters like some preachers. You and I know that you're more of a teacher and an administrator. You're sensible." Fred lifted his gaze and elevated his nose; he needed room to pontificate. "Good heavens, and after all, preachers are a dime a dozen! No need to be ashamed. You have intellect and education. You don't need emotion."

"Is there a reason why you interrupted my prayer time?"

"Now, don't get testy just because I'm speaking the truth. What I want is not so important. I can take a minute to counsel my pastor. That's what deacons are for. After all, who does the pastor go to?"

"To God. I *was* talking to God."

"Of course you were. And what did you find there in the Bible? What passage could plow your heart and bring you to tears? What do you have there?" Fred cranked his neck and leaned closer to see my open Bible.

"I was reading and reflecting over this passage." I pointed to the page. "Here, I'll read it. It's 1 Corinthians 2:3–5. The apostle Paul said,

> *I came to you in weakness and fear, and with much trembling. My message and my preaching were not with wise and persuasive words, but with a demonstration of the Spirit's power, so that your faith might not rest on men's wisdom, but on God's power.*

"God is doing something in me, Fred. He opened my eyes and my ears. I see and hear the hurting among us. People—long tormented—have come to me for relief. But I stand before them powerless to help. No wise counsel, no clever insight, no persuasive word will meet their need. I need power—the power of God's Spirit." I stood, lifted my fist, waved it in the air, and said, "I need power—just like in the book of Acts. If the Bible is true—and I know it is—then the God of the Bible is still able to deliver and do wonders today."

"Now, let me ask you something, Greg. Are these people from our church? Or are you talking about folks from the community? Outsiders? Because if you are being overwhelmed by outsiders, then maybe we should discuss this and plan a way to discourage some

## CHAPTER 11

of this. We can't have you overextended and stressed. Your preaching will suffer again."

"You don't understand, Fred. There is nothing new about these people. They have always been there—in the pew and at the door. It's just that now I notice them. I ignored them before. Their needs were too great—hopeless. Why try? But now I hear the cries. I see the pain. It's like the account of Jesus in Jericho. The crowd pressed and the people clamored for his attention. Still, Jesus heard the cries of blind Bartimaeus. The old beggar was planted by the gate—milky eyes, tin cup. He could only cry out. Still, Jesus heard and healed him.

"Jesus saw Zacchaeus in the tree. He felt the woman's desperate touch on the hem of His garment. The woman at the well argued with words, but He saw her wounds. And from across the Sea of Galilee, He heard the cries of the demon-possessed man.

"There is more, Fred. Something strange and new inside of me says, *It is possible to help them. The power is available—just ask, just seek, just knock.* But I wasn't trained or prepared for this. I feel like the disciples before the hungry multitude. Jesus said, 'You feed them!' I know it's possible. But how do I get there from here?"

"It sounds like we need a social worker on staff. Now listen, Greg, don't let this get you down. Take some time off. Rest. When it comes budget time again, I'll help you figure a way to get something extra for these folks. In the meantime, maybe you should just send them over to that Presbyterian church. They have programs to help these folks. And they're loaded. Anyway, we don't want to attract the wrong crowd."

"What?"

"You're on the right track, Greg. Don't let anything derail you. Those sermons have been just the ticket. Challenge their minds. That's what the young professionals want. And those are the families that will build this church back to its former strength."

Fred paused to survey the sanctuary. "Oh my, Greg, I remember the days when university professors and civic leaders sat in these pews. Don't you worry. We'll have that again, and I'll make sure your salary grows, too. But we need to work—and we need to work hard. After all, Greg, God helps those who help themselves."

# Chapter 12

I LET THE PHONE RING SEVERAL TIMES. I couldn't hang up. Something inside me said, *Wait for someone to answer—be patient.* It rang twice more, then someone picked up on the line. But there was only silence, no greeting, so I spoke, "Hello, Richard?"

"Hello, Richard?" A voice mimicked my words. The voice was limp and weak.

"That was my line," I answered. I wanted to sound playful—at least pleasant. "Who is this?"

"Who do you want it to be?" This time the words were hard as steel and sharp. I felt cold fingers run along my back.

"I'm calling for Richard Anderson."

"Isn't everybody?"

"Can I speak to Richard?"

"I don't know. Can you?"

"Listen, I know you're hurting. Something is wrong. Just hang on. I'll be there in a few minutes."

"You will, huh? Well, Richard won't be here then."

✦ ✦ ✦ ✦ ✦

## Chapter 12

I rang the door bell, but there was no answer. Not a sound came from inside. I knocked on the door, but no one came. Nothing stirred. I tried the door. It opened. It was mid-morning, but not inside. The curtains were drawn and the lights were off.

"Richard?" I called out. Nothing.

The sun lit the kitchen through a window above the sink. I was drawn there. The counters were cluttered, and the sink was full of dishes. A yellow pad of paper with a pen caught my eye. Among the cereal bowls, juice glasses, and spoons on the table was a note from Richard's wife. The capless pen lay on top of the note. It had been used to draw angry lines and scribbles through her words. Still, I could read what she had written.

> Richard,
>
> I'm gone! You frighten me. I can't take it anymore. If you're going to kill yourself, do it. Do something. Anything would be better than this. When you get like this, you bring everybody down. I won't live in this tomb with you. It's not right. You're not right. Don't bother me. I mean it!
>
> Vicky

I knew that Richard was in the house. I felt him.

I followed a dim hallway. A bathroom was on my right. It was dark and damp, and towels littered the floor and reached into the hall. A towel had come to rest over the doorknob. Then there was a closet. The door yawned opened. I saw linens and marked boxes and board games.

One room remained at the end of the hall. The door was opened a finger's width. A t-shirt on the floor prevented it from closing.

I knocked with one knuckle. The door inched open with each tap. "Richard? Can I come in?"

A faint, small voice answered, "By the hair of your chinny, chin, chin—you'll huff and you'll puff and you'll blow my house in." It was the same voice that had mimicked me on the phone. Childish.

The room was black—a cave, a crypt. The dim light that followed me from the kitchen was useless now. I pushed the door open and stood on the threshold. "Richard. It's Pastor Greg. I came by to see if I could help. Is there anything I can do?"

"Good question!" The reply had an edge. "*Is* there anything you can do?" I heard the sheets and bedcovers stir.

"I thought that maybe I could ... well ... uh.... If you need medication, I can go to the pharmacy or call the doctor. I could drive you to a clinic or a hospital."

"Do you think a pill or a doctor can help? Is that all you have to offer?"

"Well, no. If you'd like ... if you'll let me, I could pray for you."

Laughter erupted. The bed covers stirred like a storm. "No. Prayer won't help now. Just go away. It's better that you leave."

"Well, I can't leave you like this. I'll sit in the kitchen for a while and pray there."

"Thank you, Pastor Greg," Richard answered. He was weak but I knew it was Richard in his right mind. "I'm just not myself. I told you that I was crazy."

"Well, this darkness would drive anyone daffy. Let me turn on the lights and open the curtains."

## CHAPTER 12

"No! Just leave. Vicky was right. It's time to get this over with. Get out!" And then like a wild beast he roared, "NOW!"

"Alright! I'll go. Just relax. Take it easy. I'll leave."

I moved the shirt with my shoe and pulled the door shut. I didn't want him to hear what I was about to do. I found a phone in the kitchen and called a friend who works at the county Department of Mental Health. Dr. Stevens answered.

"This is Reverend Johnson from the First Baptist Church." I paused. I heard the phone click. *Richard's on the line,* I thought. *Hurry!* "I'm with a parishioner in his home. I'm afraid he may do himself harm. I need help."

"Does he have a gun?"

"I don't know."

"Is he mentally or emotionally unstable?" he asked.

I revealed to Dr. Stevens what I had seen.

I wondered what he thought. I knew he was listening.

# Chapter 13

"PLEASE TURN IN YOUR BIBLES TO MARK'S GOSPEL,[1] chapter five." My face perspired, my mouth was dry, and my hands trembled as I turned the pages. This felt like my first sermon. My mind was full of the thought: *This isn't a good idea. You don't know enough yet. Say you made a mistake and announce another scripture. You can preach another text.*

"They say that we teach what we need to learn. In my case, I know that's true. This sermon is proof. Please be patient. I'm no expert, just a fellow traveler. Come alongside, join me. I know that God will honor our search.

"Have you ever been in a very dark place for a very long time? Then suddenly you're thrust into the brightest sunlight? It hurts. At first you can't see. It takes time to adjust. You may need help from one who is accustomed to the light.

"I feel like I've had the spiritual equivalent of this experience. I guess I'm in good company; the apostle Paul had a similar bout.

---

1. See Mark 5:1–20 in Appendix 1.

Plus, he got knocked from a horse. Lots of others have been thrust into the light. Jacob had a ladder. It was his invitation into the light. Moses met the bush that burned and never was consumed. The glory lit his face to shining. Remember? He had to wear a veil. Then there was Isaiah—he wrote of God's brightness. Peter, James, and John tasted it on the mount of transfiguration. But Jesus never squinted. He was accustomed to the light. To him, darkness was the stranger, darkness was the lie.

"The first thing I saw in this new light was you—people. Listen to what Matthew says of the Lord's commitment to and feelings for people:

> Jesus went through all the towns and villages, teaching in their synagogues, preaching the good news of the kingdom and healing every disease and sickness. When he saw the crowds, he had compassion on them, because they were harassed and helpless, like sheep without a shepherd. (Matthew 9:35-36).

"God has given me eyes to see you in your weakness and with your wounds. He also gave me ears to hear your cries, your groans, your pleas for help. I'm sorry that I did not hear sooner. I always thought that I knew how to help you. I challenged your minds. But we don't need challenged people; we need changed people. I could challenge you, but I could not begin to work a change. I don't know how.

"So, the second thing I saw was my inability. What I needed, I did not have. I needed what the apostle Paul speaks of. He said,

> I came to you in weakness and fear, and with much trembling. My message and my preaching were not with wise and persuasive words, but with a demonstration of the Spirit's power, so that your faith might not rest on men's wisdom, but on God's power.

## CHAPTER 13

"No class, no degree, no book would give me this power. I have to press further into the light. I have to find God and know God as never before. I was happy to pray this prayer. I said, 'Lord do with me what you want.' And I believe that I heard God answer back. He said, 'I will teach you, and I will teach through you. Share the light—the truth—you have, and I will give you more.'

"I started to study these things, and God brought me to Mark chapter five. As God heard the groans of His people in their Egyptian bondage, so Jesus heard the cries of this man in Gad. And Jesus crossed the Sea of Galilee to help this one lamb, who was lost among the pigs and living among the dead.

"Even with a legion of demons within him, the man—who could not be bound—ran to Jesus and pleaded for help. He had a will to live, and, in Jesus, he had the way.

"The demons also knew Jesus, and they spoke to Him. Isn't it funny? The demons knew the Christ, and they feared him. But the religious people couldn't recognize the light that walked among them. He was someone greater than Jonah, but they did not repent. He was someone wiser than Solomon, but they did not rejoice.

"When Jesus permitted the demons to enter the pigs, the man was well, but the pigs were soon dead. And the people, who came out to see the spectacle, were more concerned for the pigs than for the person. Churches can be like that, too."

I had to take a breath. I sipped the water and scanned the congregation. Some of them sat on the edge of their pews. Their eyes were riveted to the pulpit. I felt their presence and their support. It was like family, but even greater. Then others of them were cold and dark, even hostile. They might have had a pleasant smile, but I got only frostbite. If I were to focus on them, I would stumble and stop. I found and focused on a face that was lit, and I continued.

"But Jesus didn't chide the people. He didn't say, 'Why the pigs? Why do you welcome the unclean?' Instead, he found one lost but willing sheep. This one lived among the tombs, and he roamed naked and crazed. He cut himself and cried. Scars covered his body and mapped out his misery. Outside the city limits, he could not be heard. But he was heard. Jesus heard.

"The people came out and found the man 'dressed and in his right mind.' And did the people rejoice and praise God? No. They were afraid. And they wanted God's man to leave." I left the pulpit and walked down to the floor. It's a good way to wake folks up. But I wanted more. I wanted them to be responsible for the word I was about to speak.

Once every eye had found me, I continued. "Did you know that the good news has enemies? 'Christ is born in Bethlehem!' the wise men said. But Herod offered no gift. He sent only slaughter. And what response did Jesus receive for His ministry and proclamation of good news? In Acts 10:38–39, Peter said,

> God anointed Jesus of Nazareth with the Holy Spirit and power, and . . . he went around doing good and healing all who were under the power of the devil, because God was with him. We are witnesses of everything he did in the country of the Jews and in Jerusalem. They killed him by hanging him on a tree. . . .

"In the same way, these folks in Mark chapter five didn't give thanks for God's power. They gave notice. In fear, they sent Jesus away. Fear can keep us from God's blessing. Israel chose the fearful report of the ten spies, and they suffered in the desert for forty years.

"This morning, in this place, some of you are in that desert. You relate to this man among the tombs. You feel cut off from the living and surrounded by the unclean. You cannot connect with God. Scripture is just words on a page. Prayer is something you used to do. Wise and persuasive words won't cut it. You need the power of God.

"I hesitate to say this, but I must. Here goes: I have *good news!* Jesus Christ is still alive, and His power is still at work! He knows that you are caught and crippled and cast away. He will come to you. He is Emanuel—God with us."

The people were moved. The altar filled up. *What next, Lord?* I prayed. *Tell me what to do!* Diana was unprepared for this. Her lips were pressed tight and her hands were on her hips. I'd ruined her closing hymn. I prayed in the only way I knew how. I felt feeble, but I knew that was okay. Still, I was in a strange place. I needed my brother. *Oh, Richard. I need you. Come out from the tombs.*

# Chapter 14

THE SECRETARY POINTED TO A METAL CHAIR AND SAID, "Sit here. You can't meet with him back there. I'll tell him he has a visitor. It's gonna take a few minutes. So just hang on." The monotonous, almost military directive was as cold as the room.

The chair was dented and stained with rust and spilled soda. I put my Bible on the table; it tipped like a balance. I peered beneath to discern the problem. The leveler, a folded napkin, was out of place. I used a toe to nudge it back under the uneven leg.

Richard was in an older part of the Department of Mental Health. It felt like the fifties. Tile was everywhere—on the floor, on the walls, on the counter tops. The doors were solid metal, except for the ones that were made of heavy wire mesh. They looked like parts of an animal cage. I didn't see any other clients, but the tile was quick to bring an echo of every unhappy cry.

Then from the hall nearest me, I heard a steady shuffle. Each step was short; my wait was long. I grabbed the Bible. I needed something to hold, or maybe I needed a shield. My toe caught the uneven leg. The table rocked back and banged the tile wall. There was no time to stuff the napkin back in place.

The steps were done, and there stood Richard, arms folded on his chest. His head was bowed, but his eyes were lifted. Like an old man who peered over reading glasses, he stared—unblinking—without a word.

I pointed to the other chair. "Can you sit down and talk for a while?" I asked.

"I am finished with my appointment," he said. He had that far-off look in his eyes, just like he had had that first night at the church.

"Have they got you on medication?"

"Oh, yeah. Yeah. Dr. Stevens just gave me some pills. A little paper cup filled with pills. They made me feel sorta numb. They gave me a little buzz, too. My legs shake. But the most important thing is that I don't care about nothin'. I don't think about nothin'. All I feel is cold."

"I feel it, too," I added. "All this tile makes this place feel like a—" I bit my tongue and searched for another direction. "Hey ... uh ... we had a great service this morning. I can't tell you how much I wanted you to be there."

"Uhuh," he sighed.

"What did Dr. Stevens say? Do you mind ... I mean ... could I ask you what you talked about?"

"I don't mind," Richard answered. His face was straight, but his knee began to bounce. "We talked about my childhood mostly. We talked about my mistakes."

"Mistakes?"

"Mistakes with my uncle. We would play games in the back yard. We would play doctor and patient. He told me not to tell or he would hurt my parents. I guess I believed him. I forgot all of the games. But I did keep the secret—till now. Once a doctor tried to get me to talk. The teacher said I was depressed. 'Kids aren't supposed to be depressed,' she told my mom. That only made my mom mad. She screamed and slapped me until I fell, and then she took me to a doctor. But I never told. Till now. 'Cause now I don't care. I swallowed every pill in the paper cup. He can kill me if he wants. I just don't care."

# Chapter 15

"How can I help you, Sue?"

"Well, Pastor Greg, I'm here because you were talking about me on Sunday."

"How do you mean?"

"I'm like that man among the tombs in your sermon. I can't pray. I can't read the Bible; it doesn't make sense. I feel uncomfortable at church. It was a miracle that I came on Sunday."

"What is it that you'd like me to do?"

"You know—the power of God. You talked about how words don't help and how we need the power of God. I've been in counseling two years. My money is gone, but the pain is not. I went back to the reservation—my father was Native American. I looked for answers. My answer was in Dad's old trailer. It was blue steel and cold. All six bullets were there for me. I stood in an open field and put the barrel in my mouth."

"Why, Sue? Why would you take your life?"

"What life? The only time I feel good is when I feel nothing. It gets harder and harder to be numb. Every painkiller brings another pain, and each one has a curse. My dad died from one of his painkillers. The bottle put a hole in his belly. He bled to death in that trailer."

"What stopped you?"

"Native Americans see signs where others see nothing. I guess some of that stuff rubbed off on me. I tilted my head back. I wanted the bullet to go through my brain and not my neck. But in the sky—a raven."

"Really!" I marveled aloud. "Was it a sign? What did it mean?"

"Maybe a sign. Or maybe it was just a raven. But I was told that a raven brought a message from God. I owed God a chance to be heard, but I couldn't hear Him. That's why I came on Sunday. I figured God would speak the message through you. And he did. So pray for me. Use God's power."

A spring must have popped me from my seat. I walked to the office window and searched for what to say or do next. I tried to make her understand. "Well . . . uh . . . Sue . . . I've never really . . . I mean, you're the first . . . well . . . I hate to disappoint you."

"Oh." Sue's head fell. She stared into her lap. Her fingers worked an old tissue as if it were her rosary. It was twisted and knotted and no match for the tears that flowed.

"You see," I argued, "I just started this preaching series on spiritual conflict. I'm still learning. I've only scratched the surface of the subject. Preparation and study are important to me. Some of the books are still unopened."

"I've gone to the men with the books and with the letters after their names. I've gone to them for years, but I'm no different—

only poorer. You said it was God's power. You said you couldn't get that from a book. I don't want *your* help. I want *God's* power."

I have never turned my back on a parishioner whom I counseled, but I turned my back on Sue. I peered out the window of my study, and I prayed in my heart to God. *Help me, Father. I'm lost here, and I need a way out.* Then I remembered my prayer: 'Lord do with me what you want.' I remembered the apostle Paul's words in scripture: '*I came . . . in weakness and fear . . . but with a demonstration of the Spirit's power. . . .*'

"I can't resist them another day, Pastor Greg."

"Resist who," I asked. I returned to the chair and faced Sue.

"The voices, the urges, the awful pain."

In that moment, as I faced Sue, I knew what to do. I said, "Okay, Sue. I'd like you just to agree with me in prayer. I want to ask for God's direction."

Sue bowed her head, and I prayed, "Lord Jesus, direct this time of prayer. Show me how to pray. Open my eyes and ears. Give me spiritual discernment and insight. Use me according to your plan for Sue, your daughter."

In that moment, my eyes were opened to see Sue and the powers that held her. In the Spirit, I could see her pinned to the ground—every limb anchored by these shadow creatures. Others used their hands to cover her eyes and ears and mouth. So she couldn't see her attacker or cry out for help. As these cowardly shadows held her down, a bully appeared. He kicked and mauled her until she lay mangled, bloodied, broken, and bruised.

It was painful to see. A holy anger and authority filled my chest and flowed out of my mouth. "In the name of Jesus Christ and by the power of His blood, I command any evil spirits who are coming against Sue to come to attention."

I couldn't believe the boldness and power I felt. Still, there was no response from Sue. Her head was bowed. Her hands and fingers were knitted together in her lap. She shivered and shook. I felt the chill, too.

I repeated, "In the name of Jesus Christ and by the power of His blood, I command any evil spirits who are coming against Sue to come to attention." Then I put a hand on Sue's shoulder and asked, "Are you okay? Anything happening?"

"Oh, Pastor Greg, my head. A cloud has settled in my head. A dark cloud."

I repeated my command. This time I added, "Tell me your name!"

Every part of Sue's body quivered. Her teeth even chattered. "What is happening now?" I asked.

"I don't know."

I repeated the command, "Tell me your name!"

"In my head they mimic and mock you," Sue reported. "They laugh and repeat, 'Tell me your name! Tell me your name!'"

I handed Sue a written prayer. It was a prayer to renounce ancestral sins and ancestral demons. "Please read this out loud."

"I can't. They won't let me." She was shaken and afraid. "They won't let me read this prayer!"

"Then I will read it, and you repeat it."

## CHAPTER 15

Then came a change unlike anything I've ever seen. Her facial expression, her body tone, and even her voice was changed. A sure and strong voice spoke out. No trembling. No hesitation. He turned and looked at me and said, "I am Legion. I am but one of many."

"By what right are you here?" I asked.

"I came through her grandfather. He was chief among his people. And I am a strongman."

"I command you to leave in Jesus' name!" I trembled and struggled to say the words. He only laughed.

And then another voice spoke out. It felt as if another person had entered the room. But there was only Sue, who sat before me. "I am a Power," the voice boasted.

"What right do you have to be there?" I asked.

"The gate was opened for me when she was only three. I came through her father. He was not her covering—he was her curse. Every time he exposed her nakedness and stole fruit from her body, the gate was opened wider and darkness grew. Power grew. I am a throne."

Sue's eyes formed tears and spilled them down each cheek. When he told of the molestation, her body shook as if an electric charge had surged through every cell.

"I command you to leave in the name of Jesus," I demanded.

"No!" he insisted. "I have a right to be here. I have been attached all her life. Her father let me in. I won't leave."

"I command you to go to the place where Jesus sends you!"

"I cannot. I have no place to go."

"Yes, you do. Go to the place where Jesus sends you."

## CHAPTER 15

"No!" I heard fear in the voice.

Again I cried out, "I command you to go to the place where Jesus sends you!"

"No! You don't know the harm that you will cause. If I leave this woman now, I will go into her children. You will be the gate—you will be the blame. You don't know what you're doing. You're too proud to ask for help. You have come to this unprepared and given me an opportunity to destroy this woman's life. The only good she has are those children. And you have spoiled the fruit. No, you don't want me to leave."

The words ended, but Sue shuttered and shook. Then she slumped as though she were dead.

# Chapter 16

I needed help. I needed someone else to pray. I ran out of my office and to the secretary's work area. "Sandy, where are you?" I cried out.

"I'd like to talk to you, Greg." I turned around—it was Diana.

"Have you seen Sandy?" I pleaded.

"You offended me Sunday morning. You made me look foolish in front of the entire congregation. Why can't you tell me your plans in advance? I—"

"I don't have time to talk. Please, send Sandy into my office." Then I bellowed out a desperate cry toward the other spaces of the church, "Sandy!"

I returned to Sue. She was crying. Her face was buried in her hands. Her shoulders were slumped. They rose and fell in rhythm to her sobs. "I feel so filthy, so vile. I don't understand," Sue said. She was so weak. I was afraid that she might pass out—or worse. Her skin was gray and cold.

I began to pray again. I had just begun when the door blew open. "What's wrong?" Sandy asked.

"Oh, thank God! And Daniella is with you! Please come in—both of you. Help me pray for Sue." Sandy and Daniella immediately took places on either side of Sue. Diana stood at the door. She had prevented Daniella from closing it. I had no grace in my voice. I insisted, "Please, come in or get out. But close the door."

"Something is not right, Greg. We need to talk!"

"Yes. But not now. Close the door!"

I recovered from the seismic jolt of the door closure and refocused on Sue. Daniella was already in tune with the moment. She had a way of offering comfort that could bring immediate peace. "Sandy and Daniella, please agree with me in prayer. And don't let anything alarm you. I don't have time to explain. Just trust that God is in control."

Again, I spoke to the darkness that held Sue. I commanded him to leave and to go to the place where Jesus would send him.

Sue transformed again before our eyes. The voice cackled and laughed to frighten the ladies. They each dropped their hands and stepped back. The voice said, "I cannot leave. I have no place other than her children."

"You are a liar," I said. "Jesus sends you to a place, and it is not to her children!"

Sue lost her strength and form; she was fluid. She would have spilled over and onto the floor, but Sandy and Daniella moved back in and lifted her. Each lady searched my eyes for answers. But I continued, "Release your hold on her. I command you in Jesus' name. Stop this weakness and trembling." At that moment the trembling stopped. Sue began to revive.

Once more I said, "I command you to go to the place where Jesus sends you!"

Sue lifted her head and said, "He's leaving—now." Her face changed, and a calm settled upon her."

"You must forgive the molester," I said to Sue. "When you forgive, he'll lose his hold and his rights over you."

"I know. I heard the same thing. I do forgive him. I let go of the resentment and hate." Sue extended a limp hand and gave me the twisted tissue—the symbol of her torment and tears. "It feels like morning," she whispered. Then she closed her eyes, filled her lungs, held the breath, sampled the moment, and declared, "I'm even hungry, Pastor Greg. I want toast and eggs!" Sue was weak but at peace.

"Sandy and Daniella, your prayers and support made all the difference. I grew six feet taller when you came in. Your prayers brought new strength—I could feel it. Thank you." Neither of them knew what to say. Their silence and the furrows across their foreheads told the story. I owed them an explanation. But I didn't have one—yet.

I needed time to reflect and collect my thoughts, but Diana opened the door again. "I called Fred and asked him to drop by," she announced. "I'd like him to act as a mediator to be sure that I'll be heard." Then she scanned the room and added, "Maybe you can tell us both what you were up to in here, too."

# Chapter 17

I FELT AS THOUGH I HAD GONE THROUGH A WAR. I was exhausted but excited. The day was spent, and I needed rest. "Sandy, I'm going home. If Fred comes by, offer my apology and ask to reschedule."

"Did I hear my name?"

"Fred. I was about to leave."

"I know. I heard. But this shouldn't take long, right? What's it all about? Diana called me and presumed that I knew."

"Come on. Let's take a seat in my office. Sandy will find Diana, won't you?" I looked to Sandy, and she nodded.

"Now, Greg, I don't take sides in these things. I hope you know that."

"Have a seat," I offered and pointed to the chair that Sue had occupied a few hours before. Fred didn't seem to hear me. He moved to my library and began to pull books from the shelves. He opened a few and leafed through the pages. With no thought to the order, he laid them back cross-ways on top of the others.

## CHAPTER 17

Fred continued to muse aloud, "After all, you're the pastor. I'm just one of the deacons. Diana needs to submit to your leadership. Still, God has given me a measure of acceptance among the flock. I don't know what it is. Maybe they find me accessible, easy to approach. I'm no threat. Nothing to prove, no position to protect."

I had to jump in. "Well, I can't tell you how good that makes me feel, Fred. With the pastor so aloof and unapproachable, somebody has to be there for the people."

"I have this book in my library!" Fred lifted the volume, admired the spine, and said, "My mother gave it to me when I graduated college. She wanted me to go on to seminary, said I had a pastor's heart. Dad made light of it. He said, 'Yeah, he'd make a good preacher—he's lazy and he likes fried chicken!'" Fred burst into a belly laugh. "Dad was right, of course. I was made for business—a level head and a sense for the practical."

"Well, some folks have to get real jobs, I guess."

Fred still didn't seem to hear me. My words caused him to turn around and find his seat. "I figure we all serve God in our own special ways, don't we?"

A tapping at the door announced Diana. "May I come in?"

"Well, don't you look lovely?" Fred gushed. He stood, arranged a chair for Diana, and said, "So, how can I be of help to you both today?"

Diana found her evangelistic smile and said, "It's really nothing, Brother Fred. I just thought that it would be healthy to have an objective, nonbiased viewpoint for a staff discussion we're having.

I couldn't think of any board member better suited. You have the history and a spiritual insight to draw upon."

"I need an insulin shot."

"What was that, Pastor?" Diana asked.

"Oh, nothing. Please continue."

"I'll get to the point. To prepare for Sunday, I select music on Tuesday. The choir and musicians rehearse on Thursday. We count on a consistent order of service. I'm just afraid that this last Sunday might be a sign of things to come. And I just can't bear to see any loss of the structure and consistency we've come to have in our services. Many of the choir members are at this church and pay tithe because they have the opportunity to serve through music. We have a good routine right now. Let's not rock the boat."

"Well, that was certainly painless, wasn't it, Greg?" Fred grinned and waited for me to answer, but I turned to Diana.

"I'll take your comments under advisement. Thank you for sharing. If there's nothing more, I'd like to get home. I'm a bit tired."

"Of course, Greg. But just let me say something to Diana." Fred turned to her and said, "We all appreciate your hard work and the effort that goes unnoticed by most. I know how many hours it takes to bring a choir to the level of excellence that you achieve each week. Your preparation and dedication stand as sterling examples to all of us. I recognize hard work when I see it. I can tell when a member of our pastoral staff has put in the hours necessary to prepare. And *everyone* can spot the lean times. Emotionalism and last-minute inspiration are no substitute. Isn't that right, Pastor?"

"You took the words right out of my mouth, Fred. Now, I really must be going. I promised Martha that I would change the water in the fish tank." I sprung to my feet and headed to the door. Fred and Diana didn't move. Diana looked to Fred and shook her head in disapproval. I was a disappointment. "Are you coming?" I asked.

"Oh, you won't mind if the two of us chat in your office for another moment, will you?" Fred asked.

"Of course not. And this way, you'll have the time to replace your divots in my library. Bye now."

# Chapter 18

"GREG WHAT HAS HAPPENED TO YOU?" Martha put a hand on my forehead. "Are you okay?"

"Never better—just wrung out a bit," I answered. "I came face to face with the enemy."

"Which one? Fred or Diana?"

"Well—both of them, actually. But that's not what I mean."

"Is there trouble you haven't told me about?" Martha's face went from a red flush to a white panic. "Maybe I'd better sit down."

"We contacted the other side!"

"Lutherans?"

"No! Martha, the enemy. You know, Ephesians 6: "We battle not against flesh and blood...."

"Greg, whatever Richard has—it's not contagious, is it?"

"Of course not," I said. Then I thought again, "Well, yes. It is! I hope it is. That's what we need. That's what this church needs—the power of God! Today I prayed for a woman who has seen every kind of doctor there is. Not one could save her from the torment inside. She tried to kill herself, but God sent her to me. She was

## CHAPTER 18

here Sunday. She heard hope, she heard about the power of God, and she came to me to find that power."

"Oh my! Where did you send her?" Martha asked.

"Nowhere! I made excuses and almost did send her off, but she was desperate. I figured that if God had sent her to me, then He must know what He's doing. So I prayed for God's direction, and I began to minister to her. What happened next is what I mean about 'the other side.' I believe a demonic presence—maybe more—manifested itself in that room and through this woman."

"Really? Are you sure it wasn't something else?" Martha wondered aloud. "Maybe she's a good actress. Maybe it was self-imposed hypnosis."

"The terror on her face told the story. Her body was torn and tossed like a rag doll. It was real. No one would want to revisit such shameful past abuse. She was bound and beset by these powers, unable to break free or see her escape."

"Maybe you shouldn't do this kind of prayer until you have help."

"My exact thoughts. I made no progress until Sandy and Daniella came in to pray with me. Their presence and prayers were like spinach to Popeye. I felt new spiritual muscle. That's why I want the whole church to pray! I want three days of prayer—a holy convocation. If this is some new direction or leading from the Lord, I need prayer support more than ever."

Martha squinted her eyes—a wince in the making. She asked, "Will you announce all this on Sunday? Will you mention the woman with the—well, you know? And will you explain what's going on?"

"Yes, that's right," I answered. "I've decided to continue this series of messages on spiritual warfare. I want to build a proper biblical foundation. Then after the days of prayer, if this is God . . . well . . . I mean, if it's God direction for us, I want to train others to help the hurting."

Martha stood, filled both lungs, let out a weary sigh, and said, "Well, I've grown tired of this town anyway. I'll miss many of the folks at church." She scanned the room and added, "But I won't miss this house. The kids might." Then Martha wrapped her arms around herself and shuttered.

"What's wrong?" I asked.

"Nothing," she answered. "It's just that—all of a sudden—I felt a chill"

I stood and pulled back a curtain to look out. "Maybe the weather is taking a turn."

Martha walked toward the bedroom and said without turning, "It is, Greg. I know that it is."

# Chapter 19

"Pastor Greg, before we pray today, would you mind if I just sang a hymn or chorus?" Richard didn't wait for my response. He closed his eyes, lifted his face toward heaven, and added, "You don't have to sing with me—I mean—if you're uncomfortable."

Richard began with the chorus of an old hymn:

> *I need Thee, oh, I need Thee.*
> *Every hour, I need Thee.*
> *Oh bless me now, my Savior.*
> *I come to Thee.*

His tenor voice was a calm and constant stream of sung praise, petition, and prayer. He moved from one familiar chorus to another—no seams. Each one took him farther from me and closer to God's presence.

I struggled, at first, to keep up with the songs. Then I abandoned the effort and entered the flow. It wasn't about song; it was about spirit. God's Spirit and mine—together, touching, talking.

Richard left the familiar choruses that I knew. He sang his own words of worship and adoration. It had the flavor of a chant, but more—a spiritual song or psalm. Then he cast away English altogether and sang in another tongue, a prayer language. I couldn't be alarmed or offended—it was too beautiful. But more, I felt comfort and warmth. A blanket of God's presence had covered me. I wouldn't cast it off or question it. I wanted more.

I don't remember a transition from praise to prayer. They mingled together. I found that we had begun to pray with a special discernment and knowledge. We prayed for the church, we prayed for the leaders, and we prayed for ourselves. And then Richard began to pray for me. "And for Greg, dear Lord, when the storm comes against him, give him strength. Oh, God, that he might be planted firmly in you, that his roots would sink deep into the soil of your Word, that your Spirit would refresh him, that your presence would be his refuge, where he may run and be safe."

The time of prayer and worship was done. It was time to talk. I knew that, but I didn't want to bruise the moment. God's presence was still so sweet. Richard smiled and nodded his head. He looked satisfied and full, like after a good meal.

I surprised even myself with my first words. "What was that?!" I blurted.

"Well," Richard pondered, "the Bible says that we don't know how to pray as we ought. You've been to enough prayer meetings to know that's true. So the Bible says that the Spirit prays for us and through us with special knowledge according to God's will. I guess that's what you'd call 'Spirit-led prayer.'"

"I liked the way you got us there—with song."

"The apostle Paul says, "... *be filled with the Spirit. Speak to one another with psalms, hymns and spiritual songs. Sing and make music in your heart to the Lord.* And in Psalms, David shows us the path. He says, "*Enter his gates with thanksgiving and his courts with praise; give thanks to him and praise his name.*"

"You're gonna ruin me! How can I be satisfied with the boring stuff now?"

Richard looked at me—squarely in the eyes, seriously and sternly—and said, "You don't have to be satisfied with less. It's your choice. And it's your calling."

"Richard, I need your help. You have been reinstated as youth pastor at Agape Christian Fellowship, haven't you?"

"Yes," Richard replied.

"Would it be ok if I send some of our college kids to your meetings? Also, would you give me prayer support?"

"I know," Richard answered. His head nodded agreement.

"What? What do you know?"

"I know that I'm supposed to disciple some of your college kids. And I know that you will need not just one intercessor, but many. You will need them for far more than you can imagine."

"Are you a prophet, too?"

"I'm just telling you what I see and what I hear."

"And what's that?" I asked.

"You think the intercessors are your warriors and your muscle. That's true. But you will need them in another way first."

"To lift my hands—like Moses, right?"

"No, to cover your head—like an umbrella!"

# Chapter 20

"The meeting—it's in the pastor's study, right?" Richard asked.

Diana drew back, scanned Richard from head to toe, and clutched her purse. "Yes. There is a meeting in the pastor's study. But it's only for board members and staff."

"I know," Richard answered. Then he turned his attention to the man beside Diana. "You're James, aren't you?" Richard extended a hand.

James looked to Diana, but her eyes fell to the floor. James returned to Richard and accepted his hand. "That's right. I'm James, the youth pastor. And you are—?"

"Richard Anderson. I've been praying for you."

"For me?" James gulped. "Why?"

"Because you're the youth pastor," Richard answered.

"I know that. But—your prayer? Do you pray for something in particular?"

"Pastor Greg and I meet for prayer. We pray for the congregation, the board, the staff...."

## CHAPTER 20

"Speaking of staff..." Diana interrupted and tugged at James. "We're expected in that meeting." Diana took large strides toward the study. James was in tow. And Richard, Bible tucked near his chest with folded arms, followed behind.

Diana and James entered the study. It was full. Diana waited for James to clear the doorway, and she pushed the door to shut it. But Richard had his toe just across the threshold. She put her shoulder to it, and it latched.

Then a tapping at the door. "Who's that?" I asked. "Would somebody open the door? Diana?" She was nearest.

"Of course," she answered. "Oh, Richard! I'm sorry. Was that you? I thought you understood that the meeting was private."

"Pastor Greg asked me to join you."

Then, as if none of us had heard, Diana vaulted her voice across the room. "Pastor, it's your friend Richard. He says you invited him."

"That's right, thank you. Come in and sit down." Diana and James found the only chairs. Richard stood, leaning against the bookshelf. I looked at him and said, "Everyone, this Richard Anderson. Richard has been a friend of mine since childhood. I've invited him to join us for a number of reasons. He's a real prayer warrior and has a heart for kids—"

Diana stirred and elbowed James. She had never learned to whisper. We all heard her commentary: "Start clearing your desk, James." He coughed to cover her remark and straightened himself higher in the chair.

"—but more," I continued, "Ever since Richard was a child, I could see God's calling on his life. And he has wonderful insight into the power and place of music in our worship."

This time James jabbed Diana. He wasn't any better at whispering. "Ha! Hear that? You'd better clear *your own* desk!"

I added, "These special days of prayer have transformed this place and every person who has participated."

Diana leaned ahead to Fred and murmured, "Did you know, we weren't allowed to practice in the sanctuary on Thursday? It looked like an aerobic class in there!"

"I don't claim to be a prophet," I said, "but I think it's obvious: God is changing our ministry here at First Baptist."

Fred cleared his throat, lifted his hand, and asked, "Is it all right if we ask a question or make a comment, Pastor?"

"Of course. Please do."

"Well, first, I just wanted to explain why my wife and I and the folks from our home Bible study didn't come down here and join the prayer group. Not to sound proud or anything, but we are far ahead of most in this area of prayer and intercession. I have done extensive teaching, and . . . well . . . we just didn't see the need of coming down here. Maybe we were wrong. I apologize if we missed the mark." Fred looked over to Richard and said, "Perhaps our new friend Larry brought a teaching. I'm sure it was excellent if you did."

Richard stood erect and let go of the bookshelf. He said, "Richard. My name is Richard. And there was no teaching. I was invited to come here from Agape Christian Fellowship. We joined together to pray. At the specific request of the pastor, we came to unite in prayer, as the pastor directed us."

## CHAPTER 20

"Now I see I've ruffled a feather or two. I am sorry," Fred gushed. He looked over to me and asked, "Pastor, can you find it in your heart to forgive me?"

"Of course," I answered. "Was there something else?"

"Yes," Fred answered. "Thank you. It's just this one thing that my dad used to say to me. He said, 'Son, you don't change horses in the middle of a stream.' Now, for those of you not familiar with the metaphor, just envision a man crossin' a stream on horseback. Then imagine what he'd go through to change to another horse. Well, you can see that he's gonna get all wet—at least his feet and legs."

"Your point?" I pressed.

"I'm sorry, Pastor. I'll hurry," Fred winked and showed his dental work to the others. "It's just that you said God was changing the ministry here. I don't mean to challenge anything you say, of course. Still, when I look at my Bible from day to day, it doesn't seem to change."

The group stirred a bit at Fred's comment. I heard someone say, "That's right!"

Fred continued. His Southern accent got stronger. It was his way to nudge the needle on the sincerity meter. "The gospel is pretty simple, but it's not popular. The Bible says that the preaching of the Cross is foolishness to them that perish. Now, I'll be a fool for Jesus. I don't care what others think. I don't need a change." Fred lifted his Bible and shook it—he didn't notice that six month's worth of bulletins fell out. "This Word of God is eternal and unchanging, and, so far as I can tell, so is the ministry of the church!"

Amens echoed around the room. Diana bounced in her chair.

## CHAPTER 20

Richard stood tall, faced Fred, and asked, "May I?"

Fred extended his arm to welcome Richard into the discussion. "Yes, by all means, Larry. Please share your thoughts. We're all friends here."

Every head turned to Richard. He held our gaze and used the moment to clear a silent place. Eyes closed and head lifted, he took a long breath. Then he fixed upon Fred and extended his hand for Fred's Bible. Richard held and lifted it for all to see. Sure of everyone's attention, he said to Fred, "It isn't what we've *changed* that grieves God. It's what we've *left out*."

# Chapter 21

"I'D BETTER GO. Martha will mobilize a search party soon. That was a record board meeting. I thought we might have to order breakfast."

"No, Martha knows," Richard answered. "I saw her face this morning. She knew this meeting would be no picnic. The barometer is falling, and she's already feeling the aches. If you had more sense, maybe you would, too."

"What's that mean?"

"They don't want me here."

"It is true the Board of Deacons sees you as an outsider interfering in our local church."

"Uhuh," Richard groaned.

"I don't mean the board, Greg."

"What? Diana and James? Jeepers, Richard, give 'em time. Let 'em see you're not here to take their jobs."

"I don't mean Diana and James."

"Oh, I get it. Say no more," I answered. Then I reignited with, "But why can't you see this as victory over the enemy?"

"Because the battle wasn't finished here today. It just began. My presence tips the scale. My presence will give the enemy new opportunities and open countless gates through which he will enter."

"Not through you. You won't allow that."

"I didn't say through me. It's because of me. Have you ever wondered how the enemy attaches to a life or a family or a board or a church? We, ourselves, open the gate and let him in. Whenever we feel threatened or a value is at risk, we have a choice. We can depend upon God and trust that He will protect and provide for us. Or we can leave God's camp and take control ourselves, meet our own needs. Eve's apple, Cain's murder, Abraham's Hagar, Jacob's deception, Saul's spoils, David's Bathsheba, Peter's denial, and so on.

"When we turn from our dependence upon the Father, when we leave His camp of blessing to do it ourselves, God calls this idolatry. We trust the work of our own hands, not idols made of wood or stone but idols made of manipulation and greed, resentment and anger, jealousy and hate, covetousness and lust. We put our own devices in the place of God, and we trust the created instead of the Creator.

"At that moment, when we step beyond God's camp and open the gate of disobedience, we are in their world, where they rule. Scorpions, serpents, and every scaly thing—the unholy and the unclean. For we have created a place where God is *not*. And as long as the door of our disobedience and self-reliance is open, they are free to come in and out. But believe me, once they come in. . . ."

## CHAPTER 21

Richard trembled then dropped his head. He covered his face with his hands.

"Richard, are you all right?"

"No, I'm not all right. You know that!"

"What is it?"

"For a child, his father is that covering, his father is that example of obedience and trust in God. But when a father turns from God and controls through shame or when a mother trusts in rage, a gate is opened in that young life. Those same spirits—" Richard stopped talking; only tears came. I patted his shoulder. I wasn't sure how to comfort him.

"I, too, learned to shut God out and do it myself. In time, I opened my own gates. But today, I know where to find the victory. I follow Christ and his Cross—my example of obedience. 'Turn stone to bread!' Satan said. 'No!' answered Jesus. 'My Father can feed me well enough. Not my will, but thine, dear Father.'

"So, Pastor Greg, I will be a stone of contention and an opportunity for stumbling. The folks will fear and resent me. I will be a threat. And in the face of that threat, the folks—in self-will—will rely on the work of their own hands. They will turn to gossip, murmuring, manipulation, control, conspiracy, and then vengeance and false judgment. 'Crucify him!' As they turn to these devices—idolatry, the idols they make—they will open the gates. They will create a place where God is not welcome. A place of disobedience, cold and dark and full of curses and calamity but not empty. Disobedience is an invitation. This place will be filled with the very evil they fear."

## CHAPTER 21

I shuttered and shook. My arms grew a fresh crop of goose bumps. "What is it?" Richard asked.

"Martha's ache. I just got it."

# Chapter 22

"Why are these other people here, Pastor?"

"Lydia, if you want private counseling, I can send you to a Christian therapist," I answered.

"No!" she exploded. "I've been to therapists and doctors. They put me in the hospital. I didn't get help there—I got medicine. It made me sleep all day. It was worse. The voices never left; they invaded my dreams. I was afraid to close my eyes."

"Well, then, these other folks are here to help me pray for you.[1] You and I both need them. There's no reason to be ashamed or afraid, but there is every reason to be honest. I've found that we are as sick as our secrets. The enemy uses those secrets to keep us in bondage, and he uses the shame to keep us isolated and hidden from others. But this is a safe place for you, Lydia, a place of light and love. Expose every dark corner. Give the enemy no place to hide. Do you understand?"

1. See Prayer Team in Appendix III

"No. But I don't care who knows what anymore. I just know that I can't go on like this."

"Like what?" I asked. "What troubles you most?"

"Voices in my head. Never a moment of rest. The voices tell me I'm garbage. Then I do things I don't wanta do. That's why I was homeless. I felt and looked like trash."

"What has the doctor told you?"

"Which time? Which doctor? The one who seduced me or the one who sedated me?" Lydia was intense and agitated. I looked away and whispered a prayer. The others were in prayer, hands clasped.

Lydia caught herself, "I'm sorry, Pastor. In the last six months, I've been hospitalized six times. Some doctors said I was disassociative. Others said hypersensitive or bipolar or multiple-personality." Her agitation resurfaced, and she began to rock back and forth. "I lived with a witch once. She told me I was charmed and cursed with a telepathic gift. My brother—the one who raped and abused me—said I was a tramp. My new husband—my third—calls me a loser. There were others. I've been called lots of things. So what do you think? What label do you want to give me?"

"Lydia, I do have a label for you. Please receive it and let it define you. You are a beloved daughter of God."

Lydia turned her eyes away. She shook her head from shoulder to shoulder. "No! This is silly. This can't help. No, no, no."

"Dear Father in heaven, Lydia is your daughter," I lifted my voice. "In the name of Jesus Christ, your Son and our Lord, we pray that you would set Lydia free today."

## CHAPTER 22

"No!" Lydia screamed and turned and twisted. "This is silly! None of this can help. Stop it now!"

"In the name of Jesus Christ, I command any demonic presence: make yourself known! Identify yourself!" I repeated this over and over.

Lydia began to jerk and snap and cough. "No, no, no! Stop it. I'm choking. This is silly. This can't work."

One of the prayer team members began to read Scripture aloud. Lydia's voice rose in volume to match the reader. "I'm cold. I'm cold inside. Something's not right—my chest. A heaviness—I'm choking, I can't breathe."

The reader stopped, the prayers reignited, and I bellowed, "I command any demonic presence to release this woman in Jesus' name. Make yourself known! Identify yourself!"

Lydia wrestled with the air as if she fought off a swarm of hornets. Then a still moment. Her eyes opened, but another person saw through them. The gaze pierced the chaos and confusion. Their focus was on me. I felt the violent and vulgar presence that held and harmed Lydia.

Her mouth opened, but another person spoke. The voice was coarse, cruel, and cold. "She belongs to me. This is a silly waste of time. You cannot free her. She has ruined and wasted her life. She is worthless and vile. I am just a garbage collector. Move on! She is not worth your prayers."

"That is a lie!" I declared. "Lydia is a daughter of God. She has been snatched from the fires, a treasure among the trash. She belongs to the Lord Jesus Christ. You must leave her!"

"No! She belongs to me. She was thrown away. You are wrong. No one wants her. She is trash. She knows it. And you are powerless and weak."

I'm not sure why, but I asked the Lord to send the angel Michael to help us. At my plea for help, Lydia was shaken. A beast was upon her—tortured and torn. She cried out, "No, no, no! Michael, my son."

"Lydia," I pleaded, "is it Michael the angel? Do you see Michael?"

Lydia pulled herself into a ball, her face to her knees. She sobbed and moaned and cried, "Oh, Michael! I'm sorry. I'm sorry. They made me do it. I never meant to hurt you, baby. Oh, baby. Mommy was bad, so bad."

The intercessors prayed harder. Daniella handed me a yellow pad with notes. Tears met ink, and letters ran down the page. Still, the vision was clear. Daniella expressed the picture in all of our minds: a mother and a boy, exposed and entrapped.

"Any demon of incest, identify yourself!" I command in the authority of Jesus.

Lydia's head rose. Her voice spoke for someone else. "You see, she is vile, an abomination and without value."

"What gives you any right over this woman? When did you become attached to her?"

"She was five years old. Her brother opened a door for me. She belongs to me now. There was no one to cover her or care. It is too late now; she is beyond help."

"Who are you?" I asked the demon. "Are you a principality? A throne? A ruler?"

There was no answer, but the air was foul and stale, as thick as glue, suffocating. Lydia began to choke. I spoke to the demon, "I commanded you to go to the place where Jesus would send you!"

"No! I will not!"

"Jesus is sending you someplace. Where is that?"

"To hell!"

"Then leave! Now!" I commanded. "And take all of those under your authority."

Calm covered Lydia, and peace filled the room. "How do you feel?" I asked her.

"I feel like I'm wrapped all around in a warm blanket. What happened?" She turned to look into each intercessor's face. "I was afraid of you. Now you look like friends." Her eyes fell upon the yellow tablet in Dale's hand. The word *incest* covered half the page. The word *fear* covered the other half. "Are those for me?"

Daniella placed her hand on Lydia's shoulder and said, "Not anymore, Hon. God's light has filled you today. I saw the darkness leave—all of it."

Dale tore off and crumpled up the page that Lydia had seen. He looked to her and said, "Lydia, the Lord has a lot for you—good stuff to replace the bad. If you'll let Him, God will keep you so full of Himself that the enemy will never get his foot in the door again."

Lydia reached to find Daniella's hand. She said, "I think I'll be okay so long as you folks aren't far away."

# Chapter 23

My office was still. Quiet was my company. I was hungry for the solitude. The others were off at lunch. Time alone with Scripture would nourish me.

I stood to retrieve my Bible from the place of prayer. I noticed that Dale had left his things. His yellow tablet lay on top. The crumpled page had fallen, and the page below was exposed. The words caught me. Dale had scribbled the word *clouds*, and below he had added, *Warn Pastor Greg!*

My mind raced on to search out a hundred explanations for Dale's comment. *It's related to the prayer time with Lydia, that's all*, I told myself. But I knew better. This was different. *Lord*, I prayed, *don't leave me wondering about this. What is it?*

Right on cue a *tap, tap, tap* announced someone at my door. Before I spoke, Glenda popped her head inside. "Hope I'm not a bother," she said.

"No, not at all. But what about lunch with the others?" I asked.

"It's hard to fast when chips and salsa are within reach."

"Got it," I nodded. "I appreciate your prayers. Are you worn out from the all the business we've have?"

"I've thought about unplugging that neon sign."

"What sign?"

"You know, that flashing neon arrow? There must be one out there in front of the church. Every troubled soul seems to see it. How else do you explain these last several weeks?"

"I guess you're right," I puzzled. "It seems like a hospital in a war zone—so many wounded. If we were doctors, we'd be rich by now."

"We are," she said. "At least my pockets are bulging."

"What do you mean?"

"We started this prayer team thing to support you. All of us felt that way. But once we got into it, things started to happen."

"Ain't that the truth! But what things do *you* mean?"

"It's like rich water, full of minerals. Any pipe that carries the water keeps a deposit of the wealth. Every time we serve the Lord, He leaves a little more of Himself, like the glory on Moses. I feel enriched. We haven't talked much about it, and, well, I'm not really sure how *you* feel. It's like we've received some spiritual gifts, yet we never unwrapped any presents. We just started to use what God was giving. We didn't seem to need instructions, just courage."

"What have you experienced?"

"Well, for example, Daniella has received a special knowledge about some of the people she prays for—in fact, most of them. It's almost scary, she says. Your idea about the yellow tablets has helped her express the gift. She was afraid to speak some things aloud."

"I really want her to express it. Wow, that encourages me! God teaches me more about spiritual gifts every day. The insights stretch past my experience, but that's okay; I'll catch up."

"My son Larry has been going over to that other church, Richard's youth group. I've never seen him so excited about God. I asked him about the change, and he said, 'God's real, Mom. I feel Him, I hear Him, and I know He hears me.' My husband butted in and said, 'Don't confuse emotions for faith and imagination for God's Word.'

"Larry didn't stop. He told his dad that he believed God had given him a prophetic gift. My husband jumped on that with both feet. He pulled books from his library and showed Larry how all those gifts were for another time. He said, 'Now that we have God's Word, the Bible, we don't need any prophets—especially nineteen-year-old prophets who can't even spell *dispensationalism*, let alone understand it. Larry rebutted that Jeremiah was only seventeen when God called him. He added a few things that Richard had said. That's when Harold got upset—about Richard. He said, 'I'll look into this Richard problem.' I hope he doesn't cause you or Richard any trouble."

"Don't let it concern you, Glenda," I assured her. "I have a good relationship with Harold. We'll talk it over."

"There's more, Pastor Greg," Glenda continued. "I was afraid to say anything to Larry or my husband. Larry would blab it, and Harold would bag it. But I believe that God has given me a spiritual gift, too."

"Well, I don't doubt that you have many gifts, Glenda. Anyone around here can see that."

"No, this is different." Glenda paused. She dropped her head and picked at the corner of her Bible. I sat still to let her get it out. She continued, "Please don't laugh at me or make light of this. Okay?" She looked at me and waited for my nod. "God has given me visions more than just dreams and more than just my imagination. I mean . . . well . . . visions that like . . . apprehend me, capture me and take me to the place where God wants me. In my spirit, it's a spiritual thing, I know. But after I get it, I have to share it. I mean, if I don't share, it wants to eat a hole in my gut. I gotta get it out. And I may not even know what it means. Doesn't sound very lady-like, does it?"

"You already know what Harold would say about this, don't you?"

"Yeah. He would chalk it all up to last night's anchovies or today's anxieties. These things aren't possible in Harold's mind or in his view of God and the church. At times, I wonder if he's reading from a different Bible!"

"How do you feel about that?" I asked.

"Harold is a good man, and he loves God."

"And?" I prodded.

"And he can't know what *I've* experienced. Doesn't even the Bible say that in the last days that God's people would prophecy, dream dreams, and see visions?"

I nodded and said, "The book of Joel."

"So, Pastor, what do you think? I mean, about my visions? I know I haven't shared any with you. The Lord tells me who to share with. It's kinda private. But, in theory, am I wrong? Off base?"

"The events of this last year have taught me not to underestimate God. I can't pick and choose the Bible text that suits me. I have to take it all as a whole. And God and I have already had a discussion about spiritual gifts. I told the Lord that I wanted any gift He had for me. I need His power and His presence. I'll refuse nothing from the hand of God."

"I'm glad," Glenda said. The tension fell away, and a smile covered her face. "I guess I can tell you the real reason I'm here. God gave me a vision to share with you. At first, I was afraid that my own worries spilled over, but I believe that I can trust you to discern the difference."

I reached for my pen and a tablet, something to hang on to. I grabbed Dale's and turned to a clean page. "Should I take notes?"

"No, I've already written this down for you. I'll read it and then give it to you."

Glenda retrieved reading glasses and a piece of paper from her Bible. She unfolded the page; it trembled in her hands. She read, "The Lord showed me a vision of Fred." She looked at me over the lenses and added, "You know the deacon?" I nodded, and she continued. "Behind him was a huge anvil-shaped storm cloud, a super cell like they have in the Midwest. It pulsed and flashed and grew darker and closer. Then I saw where Fred stood. He wasn't in a field back in Oklahoma or Kansas. He was at Pastor Greg's home on the doorstep." She looked up again and emphasized, "At your front door!" Glenda shuttered and shook her shoulders.

She continued, "Then I looked down and in his hand was an umbrella. There were no words spoken, but the storm spoke for everyone. It rumbled and it rocked the ground." Glenda folded the paper, handed it to me, and said, "There, I feel better. I'm sorry if you don't. I wish the vision were full of sunshine and flowers. Perhaps it makes sense to you."

My eyes fell to my lap and Dale's yellow tablet. I turned back to the first page as Glenda watched. I looked at the words and said, "Here. What do you think of Dale's notes?"

Glenda gasped and covered her mouth. Then she studied my face to read my reaction. She answered with a prayer: "Oh, dear Lord, bless Pastor Greg. Keep him safe."

# Chapter 24

"Hey, Dad," Michael rousted me from a sofa *siesta*. "Larry's dad is at the front door. He's got a briefcase. Do ya think he's selling somethin'? Want me to tell him we ain't buyin', or should I tell him you're takin' a nap?"

"No. I'll get it," I sat up, rubbed my eyes, and found my glasses. The doorbell rang.

"Good grief, Dad. What's his problem?"

"It's okay. I'll take care it."

I opened the door and found Harold wearing a suit and tie. As stern as a judge, he marched in. I intended to offer a salutation, but Harold spoke mid-stride, "May I come in?"

*You're already in!* I complained to myself.

"Well, let's get right to it, shall we?" Harold asked.

I wondered if he had a mouse in his pocket because I had no clue what he was up to. His briefcase lay opened on the coffee table. He fished out books and stacked them alongside. Hand-torn pieces of paper poked out from the pages they marked. I expected to see his calculator appear, but he closed the briefcase.

## CHAPTER 24

Harold took a moment to adjust a few books that weren't parallel to the table's edge. He pulled a pen and twisted it to expose the point. He laid it atop the clean pad of paper. The pen wasn't perpendicular to the ruled lines on the paper. He closed one eye to aim well and turned the pen two millimeters to the east. He caught and released a breath, looked at me, and began, "I apologize if my presence is an intrusion to you and your family. My schedule doesn't allow for daytime visits to the church office. Moreover, my reasons for this meeting are somewhat personal."

"Well, fine, Harold. I'm glad you came over. What can I do for you?"

"I could place these concerns on the next board agenda, but I don't do business that way. If I have something to say—I don't need to hide behind any position or a group of people to say it. Anyway—" Harold paused to wedge a finger between his collar and his neck, "—this concerns my wife and son. I'd rather keep this as private as possible."

"Glenda did mention a conversation you had concerning Larry. Didn't it have something to do with the college group at Agape Christian Fellowship?" I asked.

"I've given all of this a great deal of thought. At first, I believed that this Richard character was the source of the problem. I'm not sure now. I met with Richard, and I wasn't very—"

"Harold!" Martha called. "I thought I heard your voice. May I bring you something to drink? We're just about to have dinner. Would you like to join us?"

"No, thank you. I won't stay long," he answered.

"You must be so proud of Larry," Martha gushed. "He is so on fire for the Lord! Michael is the same way. It's like a revival among the young people. Thank God for Richard. Even Greg has learned so much from that young man. Haven't you, Greg?"

"Me? Oh, well ... uh ... I wouldn't—"

I tried to put a sentence together, but the truth distracted me. Anyway, Martha wasn't done.

"Well, you boys talk. Please give Glenda my best. Okay?"

I turned back to Harold and said, "You were saying that you met with Richard."

"Yes," Harold answered then paused. He looked around the room to find his words. Martha had knocked him off mark. He was shaken. Numbers were his domain; words were his dread. "I was about to say that I was not impressed with Richard. He is a man given to displays of emotionalism. He lacks education, stability, and maturity, things I took for granted. After reflection, and in light of discoveries here today, I've come to question your judgment, Pastor. After all, I believe you are the one who suggested our youth go to Richard's bible study at Agape Christian Fellowship."

"Well, I'm sorry that you feel that way," I responded. "I appreciate your concern and direct approach."

"You're welcome," Harold answered. "I would like to know how you intend to act upon my concerns?"

"Oh, right, of course you would," I answered. "I will pray about this and seek the Lord's direction first. I can't commit to any response until then."

"I see." Harold pressed his lips together and searched the

## CHAPTER 24

ceiling for a better answer.

"So, why the books, Harold?" I pointed to the stacks. "Don't tell me you're moonlighting as a Bible or encyclopedia salesman."

"A what?" he snapped.

"Just a joke. Why the books?"

"I intended to leave them here for you to review. I've marked the pages. Perhaps you could use them to counsel Richard." He paused to observe my reaction.

"I see." A polite smile and nod accompanied my answer.

"But, of course, if you also must pray about the books, I suppose I could take them home."

"No, I love to read and learn. It's just that I have most, if not all, of those books. Maybe you could just tell me what it is that concerns you."

"I see," Harold responded and reached for his briefcase. "I'm not prepared to argue any of the specific concerns. You are skilled in religion and rhetoric; I am accustomed to accounts and ledgers. I had hoped you would be reasonable."

Harold packed the books, replaced the paper and pen, closed the briefcase, and stood. "Glenda and Larry may be pliable and naïve, but I am not. They say I am rigid and closed. God gave us brains and reason; we don't need this ridiculous waste of time and resources."

Harold grabbed his briefcase, straightened himself, and made large steps to the door. "I hope we have a chance to discuss this again," I called out.

He didn't turn back. He spoke and walked. "We will at the next board meeting."

# Chapter 25

"Is this your hideout, Richard?"

"Oh, yeah," he answered. "I sit on one of these park benches, and I blend in with the locals—minus the brown bag."

"The ducks seem to know you."

"Fair weather friends. They disappear when the bread is gone. Still, it's fun while it lasts. Here, toss some." Richard handed me the bag of bread and added, "Try to get some to that little hen."

"Oh no! Did you see that?" I complained. "No wonder she's so puny. Those bullies plowed up, over, and through her."

"Yeah, keep tryin'," Richard urged. "In a minute she'll give up and swim off to the outside."

"I'll throw her some when she's beyond the crowd."

"It won't matter. Once she's separated herself, she won't try anymore. The bread could drop in front of her bill, in easy reach, but she won't even look at it."

"Why not?" I asked.

"Search me," Richard said with a shrug. "All I can figure is that it hurts too much to try and fail every time."

## CHAPTER 25

"Kinda sad, huh?" I wondered aloud.

"Yeah, and it gets worse. I've seen it a hundred times. In a few days, I'll find the hen over there where they nap. Not a quiet repose, nevertheless still. No head tucked under her wing. Instead, a painful sprawl—head here, wing there. It's not painful for her—she's gone. It's painful for us who have to view her end."

Richard continued, "Isn't it funny how some of us get singled out as the designated loser and outcast?"

"Did you see the wanted poster with your face on it?"

"No. Was it in the choir room, the youth room, or the board room?" he asked.

"None of the above. It was in Harold's briefcase."

"Oh. He got to you, too?"

"Yeah, but don't let it get to you," I assured.

"I won't. It's not my problem."

"Well, it's at your doorstep now, like it or not. Doesn't that frighten you?"

"No. The enemy wants me to fear. Anyway, it *was* at my doorstep; it's gone now. Heaven and hell waited and watched to see what I would do. Hell hoped that I would pick it up and fret and fix it on my own. Heaven urged me to lift it and let it go, to trust God to take it on as His project."

"Oh. So, it's not a concern to you now?"

"It's not *my* concern—it's God's. Like a drunk can't touch a bottle, I can't take control. To play God is to lose God. To scheme revenge is to forfeit rest. To doubt is to die."

"Yeah, I know."

"Pastor Greg, let me ask you something. When you see Harold, what do you see?"

"Somehow I don't think I'm supposed to say obsessive-compulsive bean-counter."

"I gave the problem to God, and God gave new perspective to me. I see Harold through God's eyes, and I love him with God's heart. I don't see a controlling husband and father. I see a man who fears loss. His wife and son have something that he doesn't have. He must dismiss their experience to defend his emptiness. Glenda and Larry have something special from God. And it's beyond Harold's reach—for now."

"You *see* his fear?"

"Fear fuels and motivates Harold. He's not the spiritual priest of his home, he's the pauper."

"And you're the problem. So how do we help him?" I asked.

"It's simple. Do you remember what Jesus told us to do with our enemies? We have only one option, you know."

"Yeah, love him."

"With God's love—like 1 Corinthians 13. That perfect love casts out fear."

"Thanks, Richard. Good lesson."

"Don't thank me. You were my teacher."

"How?"

"You loved me. The bread was beyond reach. I'd given up. But you made a place for me and invited me in."

# Chapter 26

"WHAT A TIME FOR THE DOORBELL!" Martha complained. "We have reservations, remember?"

"I'll deal with it," I said and headed for the front door.

"Happy birthday, Pastor Greg!"

"Thank you, Fred. You even have a present."

"I couldn't forget my pastor. I hope you find it useful."

"I wish I could invite you in, Fred, but we were just about to leave. It's a birthday dinner and all that."

"Not a problem. I wanted to personally deliver this gift. What I have to say can wait."

"You have more on your mind than a birthday greeting?" I asked.

"Well, it's just a tiny bit. Nothing really."

"Good, then we can—" I was cut short.

"Still, maybe I should...well...I think I should put a tiny bug in your ear." Fred looked down at his shoes. He squinted and pretended to smile—his signal for deep thought or passive-aggressive abuse. "Those of us in leadership need to stand up for one another. A little information can go a long way."

"What did you hear, Fred?"

"Well, some folks are saying that your prayer sessions are . . . well . . . a bit off base."

"How do you mean?"

"I'm not sure what the rub is. I guess a number of folks feel that you're coloring outside the lines. It's caused some concern and hard feelings."

"Who?"

"Of course, I'm not at liberty to say who."

"Well, then, I'm not at liberty to listen. Good night, Fred. My family is waiting for me."

"Pastor, I don't want you to think I'm upset with you. It's clear that this fellow has taken advantage of your kindness and abused your friendship. You needn't defend him on my account."

"Do you mean Richard?"

"Yes, of course, I meant to say Richard. But my point is that even the best of us have our lapses in judgment. It's nothing to be ashamed of. The harm would be in letting this continue."

"I'm not sure what you're driving at, Fred."

"Well, look at it this way. You can't sew silk and burlap together and hope to get a useful garment. It doesn't mean that the burlap doesn't have its place. It does—it is useful, but in it's proper place."

"I'm confused, Fred. Am I the burlap or are you?"

"Well, I was referring to Richard, of course. You see, he has a place at Agape Christian Fellowship. That doesn't mean we should encourage our youth to be influenced by him."

"Just for the record, Fred, I have confidence in Richard. The Lord brought him back into my life for a purpose. He has been my closest friend in the last several months. He has taught me far more than I ever taught him. If he is off base, then so am I."

"Now, Pastor, I find it hard to believe that a man of your education and experience could give a nod to the foolishness that's been reported."

"What's been reported?"

"Well, I hesitate to say what I've heard. It borders on the . . . well . . . absurd. It's lunacy."

"What is it?"

"They say you lock up mentally ill or emotionally unstable people and pray for them until they charade around like demon-possessed fools. You carry on conversations with these crazed folk until they claim to be delivered of their evil spirits. Now, that's right off the stable floor, and I just can't believe that!"

"I'm glad you can't believe it. It's only partly true."

"And the true part?" Fred asked.

"We have prayed for people with life-controlling problems. And we have discovered demonization. It has even manifested itself in our prayer sessions."

"Greg, you can't be serious. The Bible referred to demons because of the superstitions and ignorance of the people. We know today that it was epilepsy or some other common problem, not spirits. Demons or bogeymen have no place today."

"I'm sorry, Fred. The Bible says that Jesus spoke to the unclean spirits. He wouldn't have spoken to epilepsy."

"He also spoke to the waves, Greg. You don't see me talking to my water glass."

"I need to go, Fred. Perhaps we can discuss this again in my office."

"Of course, Pastor. Until then, I'll just keep this between you and me. No one else needs to be alarmed. Once you end your relationship with Richard, you'll come around."

I had to restrain myself. I wanted to reignite and launch a new argument. Instead, I said, "Good night, Fred. Thank you for the birthday present."

"You're welcome. If the almanac is right, you'll need it."

"Why's that? What is it?"

"Storms are coming, Pastor. I got you an umbrella."

# Chapter 27

"Sandy, what's wrong? Is the church on fire?"

"It feels like it. I had to get out of there. I'm so glad you're here, Pastor." Sandy sat at a picnic table near the church playground. She put her elbows on her knees and her head in her hands.

"What is it?"

"Diana and Richard. She has nipped at his heels for days. I don't know how he's stood it. He had it up to his gills. I can't blame him for what he said."

"What did he say?"

"Well, first, she said he poisoned some of her choir members against her. The college kids in his group have gotten into worship and some spiritual things. They made suggestions to Diana—quoted some Scripture. She said it was mutiny."

"What did Richard say?"

"Richard said that it wouldn't hurt her to listen to the young people. He said she might learn something."

"Oh, oh."

"Yeah. The next thing I knew, Diana threw all her photocopies like confetti. There are pages of sheet music all over the floor in my office. It's a mess in there. Then she lost it. She screamed, 'How dare you patronize me! I'll have your butt fired in a week. No one will take my church away from me. Do you understand that, you psychotic sick-o? Why don't you go back to *your* church?'"

"What did Richard say?"

"Nothing. He just left. I felt real bad for him. Is there anything I can do?"

"Yeah. You can pray for me. I don't mean that in a philosophical way, either. Put the phone on the answering service and pray for this situation. But first, call a few of the others and ask them to pray. Don't even explain anything. I don't want to give the enemy any opportunity for gossip or division. Maybe the Lord will give them some insight."

"I'll bet Diana is burning up the phone line right now."

"That's her choice. I'd rather that we communicate upward. You call the intercessors, and I'll check on Richard."

"Oh, but, Pastor," Sandy called back.

"What is it?"

"I don't know if I should say anything to you. After all, it was hearsay, and this situation is bad enough."

"If it's gossip about another person, I'd rather not—"

"Oh, no, nothing like that. It's just that ... well ... did you know that there was a board meeting last night?"

"No. There couldn't have been. Nothing was scheduled."

"I heard that it was at Fred's place."

"Last night was his Bible study group."

"Right, but it was also attended by all the board. I overheard Diana say it was a 'strategy meeting.'"

"Even Dean? Do you know if Dean attended?"

"I heard that *all* the board was there."

# Chapter 28

"Can I come in?"

"Aren't you supposed to say 'May I'?" Richard asked.

"Oh, right. May I come in?"

"I'm sorry. Don't you hate that, you know, when people correct your English? My life has been full of umpires. They call balls and strikes on my every move. I'm tired of the game. It's no fun anymore. Why can't I just hit the ball and run the bases?"

"That's why I like football?" I interjected.

"What?" Richard puzzled.

"Sorry to mess up your metaphor," I answered. "But I like football 'cause I can always hit somebody!"

Richard smiled. Then he chuckled. Next he surrendered to a lap-slapping belly laugh. He recovered and said, "Thanks, I needed that."

"I saw the fur all over the office floor. I guess I just missed the cat fight. Sandy clued me in."

"Yeah," Richard sighed. "It was a little messy. Diana believes that I've turned her college-age choir members against her. And there's more to it now."

"What do you mean?"

"Well, I got a call this morning from Fred. He asked to meet with me. He said that he and two other board members would like to meet with me."

"About what?" I asked.

"About my influence on your college age kids, I guess. They want to correct my heresy or burn me at the stake."

"Man, you were right about being a stumbling block to these folks. Rather than seek God's will, they turn to all sorts of childish tricks."

"Let's be clear," Richard cautioned. "They turn in self-will to their own devices. Outside the camp of God, their rebellion is a welcome sign to the enemy. He sees their 'childish tricks' as an opportunity for control—an occasion to defeat the good work God has begun here. The air is already thick. It's like a call has gone out. They smell blood."

"What do we do?"

"We go to the rock; we stay close to God."

The door opened, and I jumped. It was Sandy. "Sorry to startle you," she said.

"It's okay. What's up?"

"I asked the intercessors to pray and to write down any instructions or impressions that the Lord gave them during prayer time. All of them have called back. There seems to be a common word from the Lord. He says to join together for prayer in the sanctuary. Glenda added that the Lord wants to show us the enemy—not for fear, but focus."

# Chapter 29

"I'll open in prayer," I said to the group of intercessors. "Then, I'd like Richard to lead us in a time of praise and adoration. The Lord will direct us after that."

I prayed, and Richard picked up his guitar. He tuned the strings and said, "Do you know how they train Secret Service agents to spot a counterfeit bill? They immerse them with the genuine article. They know everything about real currency. So when a phony comes along, they nail it.

"The Holy Spirit has instructed me to immerse myself in God's Word, in God's presence, and in God's work. And that work doesn't have to be a paid ministry position. I can serve God wherever he plants me. The Holy Spirit wants me so close that I can hear His instruction, obey His voice, and see the truth. Don't focus on the problems here tonight—focus on the presence of the problem solver."

The worship and praise lifted my head. A peace melted the tension in my neck. In a crescendo of praise, I felt the Lord's presence, I sensed a sweet aroma, and I knew a company of angels had joined us. A wave of joy flowed over the folks who sang and praised. The warmth and peace that settled brought courage and confidence. God was among us, and He would provide for us and protect us.

I looked to Glenda and said, "I believe the Lord has given you something to share. What is it?"

Glenda lifted her voice, "As we walk around this sanctuary—in God's Spirit and with His purpose—the Lord will reveal the nature of the battle we face."

"Well, then, let's turn to prayer," I said. "Walk around the sanctuary. Write down the impressions and insights God gives. We will come together in a while to share and conclude."

Richard sat on the steps that led to the platform and pulpit. For several minutes he faced the pews in silence, eyes closed. He stood and walked to the baptismal. He laid a hand upon it and groaned. Then he returned to the steps and remained there.

I called the group together and asked them to share. Daniella walked to an area in the sanctuary and said, "Deception sits here."

Glenda swept her hand over a section and said, "Pride is empowered here."

"What else have you sensed?" I asked.

Richard stood, walked back to the baptismal, placed his hand upon it, and said, "Murder. Blood cries out for justice. Murder has been here."

One of the college-aged girls stood and walked to the place Daniella had pointed out. She didn't attend Sunday services, just the college activities. I was interested to hear her insight. "I can't say that I heard any name or saw anything evil here. But this spot is cold. It gives me the creeps. I feel invaded, like someone is staring at the back of my neck. It's a violation. What is it about this spot?"

"That's where I sit, of course." The sanctuary doors were wide open and Fred was now among us. Harold was just behind him, and Diana at his side.

Fred was different. There was steel in his walk. He stood before Richard and said, "Why are you in our church?" His tone was cold and cruel.

Richard sat still. He lifted his face to Fred and said, "Your pastor invited me."

"I don't believe you. You can fool these others, but I know you. I know what you're after."

"Maybe I can help, Fred," I offered.

Fred turned a stern glare toward me and growled, "Haven't you helped enough? If you'd done your job right, I wouldn't have to clean up this mess."

"What makes you think you have to get involved at all?" I countered.

"This is *my* church. My family built this church. My family donated this land. My grandfather's business was here, right here." Fred stamped his foot to punctuate, and he pointed to the front. "His office was over there, right where the baptismal stands. So don't tell me I can't get involved. I am involved."

Richard stood and faced Fred. "I'm sorry, Fred. Perhaps I should not be here. I apologize. How can I make it right?"

"There's still time. Come with us." Fred turned and walked out, Diana and Harold in tow. Richard followed.

## CHAPTER 29

Richard stopped and looked back. I said, "I'll be there in a minute."

He shook his head and said, "No. They just want one—for now. You'll have your chance soon." He lifted his voice louder for the whole group and said, "God has shown you the enemy tonight. It is not the flesh and blood you see, but the powers behind. Aim well."

# Chapter 30

Richard would not enter the sanctuary again.

I called a board meeting for Sunday after church. Daniella, who had given herself to fasting and prayer, said that she would pray in the ministry room during the service. I needed all the help I could get.

Diana was all bubbles and fizz. Her threat was gone, but my brother was missing in action. I didn't want to be there. The sermon fell flat. I think I read it word for word.

Next was the board meeting. All of the deacons were seated. No staff members were present; it was an executive session. I did not have the discernment that the intercessors demonstrated. Still, I could read each face. I had only one friend among them: Dean. And he had been a party to all of this.

"You don't have the right to tell our youth where they can and cannot go!" I began.

"We do have that right!" Harold answered.

"What happened to Richard?" I asked.

## CHAPTER 30

Fred looked to each deacon with his characteristic display of dental work. "I'll answer for those of us who counseled with Richard." He watched for and received the nods he wanted.

"Well," Fred began, "several pieces of sensitive information about Richard surfaced. I felt it was best to contain that information within the smallest circle possible. We did not want to accuse wrongly or cause undue embarrassment to the parties involved. When Richard was confronted with these things, he felt it was best to instruct the college age youth not to come to his bible study again."

"What pieces of information do you have?" I demanded.

"I don't think it's necessary to disclose it to you, Pastor. Believe me, we are protecting you."

Dean spoke up, "Tell Pastor about Wayne's son."

"Well, alright," Fred nodded. "It seems that Wayne's son Keith confronted Richard about some of his teaching. Richard claimed that God gave him a special gift—a word of knowledge, I believe. He said that he knew things about some young people in his college flock, secrets that God had whispered to him. He said that it was to help him pray and minister to those lost or wandering sheep.

"Keith spoke up and asked, 'Has God told you something about me?' Richard said, 'Yes.' So Keith said, 'Spill it. Right now in front of everybody. 'Cause I don't believe you.'

"Without batting an eye, Richard said, 'You are sleeping with your girlfriend, and the Lord is not pleased.' Well, to say the least, Keith was shocked and his girlfriend was embarrassed. In any event, that caused a few people to worry about Richard. One parent felt we might have a voyeur on our hands. A little research turned up several insights about Richard. He has a history of mental illness."

"So you threatened to expose all of his secrets?" I asked.

"Of course not. We discussed a number of options. I, for one, am very satisfied with the outcome. I can see now how his mental illness gave rise to all of these fantasies about prophecy and spooky gifts and supernatural healing."

Wayne interrupted and said, "I told him to get a job at the psychic hotline." Everyone but Dean laughed.

"So, Pastor Greg," Fred continued, "I'd suggest that you let this storm pass. Rethink your opinion of Richard and some of his ill-advised teaching. Time will help you see more clearly. Like my father used to say, 'Time heals all wounds—or wounds all heels!'"

"I can assure you that I will pray about this," I responded. "I will rethink the teaching. Richard might have been zealous, but I don't think he was reckless or wrong. Still, I will have an open mind. You will get to hear the result of my study and prayer next Sunday morning. I think the whole church should hear my discoveries and conclusions."

"Good! Good, Pastor," Fred gushed. "I know that sensible Pastor Greg will study and sort through all this and bring us a challenging message next week."

# Chapter 31

"This morning's sermon will be different. Maybe more of a talk from my heart. You see, I've spent a lot of time this week in study and prayer. I promised the board that I would look into this topic of spiritual gifts and other New Testament manifestations of the Holy Spirit.

"In all of the materials, I found two schools of thought. One believes that these gifts and manifestations were for the time of the apostles. They were to give credence to the New Testament writers, signs of their authority. But once the Scriptures were written and the church was established, the signs would cease.

"On the other hand, others say that the signs and wonders are still expected and appropriate today. Whatever occurred in the New Testament can and does happen now. They quote the Scripture found in Hebrews 13:8, *'Jesus Christ is the same yesterday and today and forever.'*

"Listen to the last verses of Mark's gospel:

> He [Jesus] said to them, 'Go into all the world and preach the good news to all creation. Whoever believes and is baptized will be saved, but whoever does not believe will be condemned. And these signs will accompany those who believe: In my name they will drive out demons; they will speak in new tongues; they will pick up snakes with their hands; and when they drink deadly poison, it will not hurt them at all; they will place their hands on sick people, and they will get well.'
>
> Then the disciples went out and preached everywhere, and the Lord worked with them and confirmed his word by the signs that accompanied it.

"I would be afraid to edit the words of Jesus and add a time limitation. The apostle Paul talks about spiritual gifts in 1 Corinthians—everything from healing and helps to prophecy and wisdom. I see no time limitation there, either.

"I think it comes down to faith. We experience God and His gifts according to our faith. Often, we are like Mary and Martha, the sisters of Lazarus. Remember how Jesus waited until His friend was dead?

"Jesus arrived on the scene, and Martha met Him. Her faith was in the past. She said, *'Lord, if you had been here, my brother would not have died.'* You see, she could believe in signs and wonders, but in the past tense. Some folks today believe in miracles—the ones that happened years ago in the Bible. But they can't believe for miracles in the here and now.

"When Jesus said, *'Your brother will rise again,'* her faith leaped ahead to the future. She said, *'I know he will rise again in the resurrection at the last day.'* She could believe in the miraculous, but not for today. Many folks tend to put all of their hopes on the second coming of Christ.

"To the hungry they say, 'One day, when Christ returns, we will eat freely of the manna of heaven. There will be no want then.' To the sick they say, 'Life is tough, but one day there will be no sickness or disease.' To those who suffer injustice they say, 'One day, Christ, the righteous judge will return and set things straight.'

"Their hope becomes a postponement for the hurting. They focus so much on the Second Coming because they are trying to deny the implications of the first coming!

"I know that some would have me live and teach the faith of Martha. Believe that it did happen and believe that it will happen, but don't believe that it *does* happen.

"I like the town, the parsonage, and the salary, and you folks have been good to us. But I cannot teach and preach to you about an impotent Jesus who is unable to help His people. I must teach and preach to you about the imperial Jesus, who is King of kings and Lord of lords. He is Lord over death and hell and the grave. He is Lord over disease and poverty and every evil thing. He is able to save you both now and forever. Nothing can separate you from the love of God in Christ. Nothing!

"So, I would like to announce that where Richard left off, I will pick up. Next Sunday, I will begin a series of messages about spiritual gifts. The first message is titled "Spiritual Gifts for the Here and Now—How to Unwrap the Present."

# Chapter 32

THE INTERCOM SOUNDED A TONE, and Sandy's voice followed. "Pastor, Dr. Haynes and his friend Sean are here."

"Please show them in."

Sandy opened and the door to my study. Dr. Haynes and Sean entered and found seats. "Have any of the intercessors arrived?" I asked.

"Glenda is already in the prayer room. She came early to have the room to herself for a while. I'll let you know when the others are there." Sandy stepped out, but she stopped short and said, "Oh, I almost forgot. I have a phone message from Fred. I'll get it."

"No. Just tell me what it was," I urged.

"Are you sure?" she cautioned.

"Yeah, Doc Haynes knows a bit about our craziness around here."

"He said it was about Sunday's message. He apologizes for leaving the service before the benediction. He said he had to retrieve a name and phone number for you. He said you would need it."

"Did he give you the name and number?" I asked.

## CHAPTER 32

"Yes, I'll bring it in later."

"Who was it?"

"It was a number for Mr. Speedy's Resume Service."

"Oh my!" Dr. Haynes gasped. He removed his hand from his mouth and said, "I'm sorry, Greg. I didn't mean to react."

"That's alright," I answered. "Nothing surprises me anymore. Maybe we can talk about it later."

"I'd be happy to."

"Enough about my stuff. How can I help you gentlemen?" I asked.

"Well, Pastor Greg, I suggested to Sean that we see you. He has been in therapy with me for about six months. I explained that we refer folks to one another. Still, he wanted me to join him on this visit. He has anxiety about the sanctuary. I explained that we'd be in your office or a side room. I hope you don't mind if I stay while you counsel and pray with Sean."

"If it makes Sean more comfortable, I'm all for it." I looked to Sean, but he had not yet made eye contact with me. He focused on Dr. Haynes or his own knees. Both hands were under his thighs to warm or settle them. Sean was never still. He blinked hard or bit his lips or shook his head to unwind his neck. He bounced one knee and then the other. He twisted often to look at the door or a corner but never at me.

"How old are you, Sean?" I began.

Sean looked to Dr. Haynes. His face was drawn up tight. Forehead furrowed, eyes squinted, lips pressed tight. "Sean is just about thirty," Dr. Haynes said. "It's hard for him to put his thoughts together. He says his mind races faster than he can talk. He gets embarrassed when people don't understand him."

Dr. Haynes looked at Sean and said, "I'd rather not speak for you, Sean. Pastor Greg is a good guy. Don't be afraid. He wants to help."

Sean lifted his head and found my eyes. "I'm twenty-nine, but I won't see thirty."

"Why do you say that?" I asked.

"I just know. Drugs—the hard life. A fortune teller or psychic—some death card—she told me. I'm dead already." Sean took a deep breath and returned his gaze to his knees. Both bounced now.

Dr. Haynes placed a hand on Sean's back and encouraged him. "Thank you for sharing that, Sean. Anything else you'd like to say to Pastor Greg?"

"Voices—you know. Everybody's got 'em. Aaah ... well ... I just know. ... I mean, I can't lick. ... They been there since I was a kid. You know?" He lifted his head and waited for me.

"I'm sorry, Sean," I offered. "It must be painful." He nodded his head and leaned over his knees. "Can you remember when this began?"

"I was ten. A seance. My sister and some lady. I needed guides. The voices were supposed to ... uh ... well ... you know ... uh ... help me. If I listen, they tell me— Like today, I'm not supposed to be here. Lots of warnings."

"Are you anxious about being here?"

"Big time!" he answered and shook his head up and down. "I know stuff before it ... uh ... you know ... like before it happens."

"Do you have feelings about today?"

"Oh, yeah! Not a good time. Maybe . . . uh . . . next week or who knows."

"No, Sean. We're gonna stay here and see if Pastor Greg can help." Dr. Haynes was firm. "According to you, you might not be here next week."

Dr. Haynes looked to me and added, "His birthday is Saturday."

"Yeah!" Sean bellowed and laughed. "Yeah, that's the idea." It was a different Sean. He mocked and laughed.

"Well, Greg," Dr. Haynes began, "do you think you might be able to help Sean with any of this?"

Sean shook his head east and west, smiled broadly, and repeated, "No, no, of course not. There's nothin' left of me to save."

"No, I disagree, Sean. I might not be able to help you, but I know that God is able. Please let us pray for you and with you."

"I'm allergic to prayer," Sean shot back. "What does she want?"

"Who?"

I didn't finish my question before Sandy put her head in and said, "The others are in the prayer room. You can join them any time."

"There are a few folks I'd like you both to meet."

"I won't go in the church," Sean demanded.

"That's fine. We can enter the other room from an outside door. Follow me."

I led Dr. Haynes and Sean out of my study and toward a side door. Then a sharp voice from behind stopped me cold, "Wait, Greg, don't forget Mr. Speedy, the resume service."

*Oh, Lord,* I prayed, *not Fred—not now.*

## CHAPTER 32

I stopped, turned, and prepared to deal with Fred. But there was no Fred. Dr. Haynes at the rear and Sean at my heels. "Who was that?" I asked.

"Not me," Dr. Haynes answered. "I didn't hear anything."

Sean locked eyes with mine and lifted one brow. A smirk covered his face—a shrug lifted his shoulders. "I heard it," he said. "You're not crazy. Not yet."

# Chapter 33

I OPENED THE DOOR and flooded the prayer room with sunlight. Glenda, Dale, and Louise were in prayer, yellow tablets and Bibles in their laps or under their chairs.

"Well, well, this is no prayer room!" Sean boasted. "This is the nursery! Ha!"

"Oh, Greg," Dr. Haynes interrupted and motioned to me. "I forgot my date book and notes in your office."

"Introduce yourselves to Sean," I said to the intercessors. "I'll be back in a jiffy."

"Liars go to hell, Greg," Sean hissed. "Now, tell the truth. You're just going to talk about me behind my back."

I stepped outside with Dr. Haynes and closed the door. "Now, see, Greg? Notice that change in personality there in your study and here now?"

"Are you familiar with that?" I asked.

"Yes, of course. That's what led to a diagnosis of Multiple Personalities, the M.P.D. I mentioned."

"But you don't sound so sure."

## CHAPTER 33

"I've known Sean for years, off and on. I worked for the county years ago. I met him first in juvey. I saw him at the request of the court and probation. Back then, he was just a hyper kid with tics and a temper. Sean was sweet. I could connect with him. I thought I understood his trouble. But even then there was something else. I mean, I could see that Sean was being crowded out."

"Crowded out?"

"Yeah, you know. Like an overbearing mother or older sibling who answers for you, and tells you what you want. I figured it was that internal, critical parent we all have. Still, I just couldn't be sure."

"Have you asked Sean about it?"

"Yeah," Dr. Haynes paused, looked off, and nodded, full of his own thoughts. "Sean said, 'I'm nothin', I'm nobody. Maybe I made a deal with the devil. You know, so I could be somebody.'

"Greg, he's convinced himself that he did ... you know ... make a deal. He said the devil has taken Sean away bit by bit—on the installment plan. Last week, he said, 'There ain't hardly nothin' left of me. It's almost all them now. And they'll have it all before I'm thirty.'"

I motioned toward the door and said, "We'd better get back."

Sean leaned over into his lap, hands over his ears. The intercessors were quiet, but their eyes were wide and glued to Sean.

I didn't waste time. I positioned myself and began to minister to Sean. "I ask you, Lord Jesus Christ, that you will separate all demonic from human parts of Sean, and I command the demonic to leave Sean and go to the place that Jesus sends you."

## CHAPTER 33

Sean sat up. He trembled, fear in his eyes. It was the awkward Sean who had first spoken in the office.

Again, I confronted any demon that had come against Sean. He shuttered and closed his eyes. "What is it Sean? What do you see?"

"One of them is on a throne," Sean said. "It's like… you know … like a cartoon. It has a scepter; it's huge."

I commanded the demon to leave and go to the place Jesus would send it. But it spoke through Sean and said, "You have no power over me. I have authority to be here. He belongs to me."

"By what right do you claim him?" I asked.

"He invited me in. Since age ten, he has belonged to me. It happened in the seance. He pleaded for my help. You have no power. He wants me."

I demanded to speak with Sean. I asked him, "Do you see others around the throne?"

"Yes," Sean answered. "I see six others."

"Who are they to you, Sean? How do you describe them?"

"They are who I am now. They say they fill my life: deception, terror, rage, hatred, worry, lust. They say that if they leave, there won't be anything left." Tears streamed down Sean's face. He cried out, "I'll die."

"What has lust moved you to do?" I asked.

"I've had three affairs. Three women—all married. I seduced them."

"In the name of Jesus Christ, I command the demon of lust and adultery to go to the place that Jesus sends you."

A cruel and angry voice bellowed from Sean, "You coward! Come back! He is ours."

In the same way, the others were cast out: deception, terror, rage, hatred, and worry. Deception left, and Sean's demeanor changed. Dr. Haynes saw it. He stood to his feet and cried, "Sean, there you are. I knew you were still there."

The throne demon called the others cowards. Still, each one left. The remaining demon appealed to Satan for help.

I told him, "Now, only you are left. Go to the place where Jesus sends you."

"No, I was the first. He relies upon me. He does not chose to let go. I will remain."

I demanded to speak to Sean. I asked, "Who is this throne? What is he to you, Sean? Do you want to be freed?"

"His name is Violence," Sean answered. "I want to be free, but I'm afraid. How will I live? What will I do? Who will I be?"

"You will find a new identity, your true God-given self, in the Lord Jesus Christ. You'll find family and acceptance and love among God's people. But you have to let go, Sean. Do you have a violent temper?"

"Yes," he answered.

"Do you want to be released from it and forgiven?"

"Yes." Sean wilted and swayed. He had no strength to speak.

"Stop it!" Violence demanded. "You may no longer speak to him. He's mine." Then he exploded with force and anger, "Get away from me, preacher man! You are too weak to deal with me. I've heard of a coming revival, but where is it? Ha!"

## CHAPTER 33

"Dear Lord Jesus, rise up and battle in our behalf. Send your angels to free Sean. You, Oh, Lord, set the captives free. You bring release to the prisoners. Save and set free this dear one. Send your angels to war in our behalf."

"Stop it! Get away!" Violence screeched and howled.

Dale lifted his yellow tablet. He wrote that God had given him eyes to see the angels come. His vision coincided with the demon's screams. He wrote, AS WE PRAY, THE ANGELS LEAVE. THEY GET THE PRAYERS AND RETURN WITH MORE POWER.

Louise lifted her tablet. She wrote, MORE PRAYER NEEDED. Glenda read it, nodded, and ran to the office. She returned with Gina, who had prayed with us, but not for a person like Sean. Glenda wrote, SANDY WILL CALL PRAYER CHAIN—COMMUNITY FELLOWSHIP—ABUNDANT LIFE.

We prayed, and the demon thrashed Sean. He was a leaf in a storm. We read Scripture, and the demon threatened harm to Sean. Glenda began to praise. It touched a nerve. Violence was enraged, and his volume was deafening. Dr. Haynes stumbled backward, his handkerchief over his mouth.

We all joined Glenda. We sang and spoke our praise. We grew louder than the demon. Praise and exaltation for Jesus filled the room, the demon had no power. Dale saw him get up from the throne and leave.

"Sean, now is the time to invite Jesus to sit on the throne," I said. "Will you do that?"

He prayed, "Yes, Lord Jesus Christ, sit on the throne of my life. I invite you in. Fill me. Replace the evil. Restore the good. Heal me."

Dale said, "I see Christ upon the throne of Sean's life. Jesus asks us, 'Do you want to see the man totally free?'."

"Yes, Lord, please," everyone spoke.

Then Sean began to make all types of renunciations without anyone prompting him. *How does he know to do this?* I marveled. Moments earlier, he was controlled by evil. Now, he speaks by direction and unction of the Holy Spirit. I could only thank and glorify God. *Praise you, Jesus! Thank you, Father! Come Holy Spirit!*

I wasn't prepared for what happened next. The presence and power of God's Spirit filled the room. It electrified and intoxicated everyone present. I was dazed. It was God's *energeia!* A manifestation of the Holy Spirit. I felt electricity come over my head and move down my body. I had never felt so much power and joy.

I looked to Sean. He transformed before my eyes. Peace poured over him, but it didn't stop. It overflowed to the room. My knees lost strength and found the floor. The others were overwhelmed, weakened with awe. Glenda knelt. Dale was prone, his face to the floor. Louise sat in a chair, her hands lifted. No words matched my emotions or this experience. The Lord had walked among us. I didn't know that was possible.

When God's glory left the room. Dr. Haynes was seated on the floor, his back to the wall and his mouth dropped open. He tried to speak but had to gulp and cough several times to find his voice. When he could speak, he cried out, "What was that?!"

Sean spoke for us all. He said, "That was God."

"How are you, Sean?" Dr. Haynes asked.

"I am … well … I am *clean,*" Sean answered. "I felt the broom of God's Spirit sweep me clean. Every dark corner is clean."

I didn't have the repose or presence of mind to answer Dr. Haynes or to respond to Sean. Like someone after a "close call," I checked myself all over—to see if I was still there. I was okay, but something had happened to me. And I would forever be changed.

# Chapter 34

THE NEXT DAY, I WAS BACK IN THE PRAYER ROOM. Alone. Numb. Still awe-struck.

"Pastor, it's your wife on the phone. She wanted to remind you about your guests from San Diego. They just arrived at your home." Sandy spoke from the door. I knew she was there. I just couldn't manage an answer. She came all of the way in and said, "Pastor, did you hear me? Do you want me to call Martha back?"

"Oh, I'm sorry." I shook myself and focused on Sandy. "Yes, right . . . I mean, please call Martha and ask her to bring Tyler and BJ to the church." Sandy stood in the middle of the room. She extended her hands as if feeling for heat. "Sandy?"

"What's happened in here? What is it I feel?" she asked.

"Oh, good. I'm glad you feel it, too. And you weren't even here yesterday."

"I'm serious, Pastor. What is this?"

"I can't describe it, Sandy. All I know is, that yesterday at the end of our prayer time for Sean, God's glory filled this room in . . . well . . . biblical proportions. I came back today to reflect on the experience. I was shocked to still feel a measure of it. I guess it takes time to fade, like Moses' face."

"Huh?" Sandy grunted and sat down. Her face was pinched by the puzzle. "Years ago, I went to the theater to see the great Bible movies. I was just a kid. At the end of each film, I felt an awe. I wanted to get saved all over again. I felt like I was in the presence of something great, like when you're next to the Grand Canyon, one of those huge planes at the air show, or maybe the president. I experienced fear, yet I wasn't afraid. I'm not making sense, am I? Anyway, I feel like all that right now."

"Maybe we should sell tickets," I spoofed.

"What?" Sandy was still lost in the puzzle. "Oh, right. I'll get right on it. I'll call Martha."

Before Sandy stood, I heard someone outside the door. It was opened a crack. His voice invaded the moment, but his presence couldn't diminish the atmosphere.

"Speaking of calls, Sandy, did you give Pastor my message?"

"Yes, Fred," Sandy brushed her hands on the apron she didn't have and slid past Fred. He came in and took her seat, the very seat Sean had occupied the day before.

Fred faced me and rubbed his hands together like a glutton before a feast. I knew I was the main course. He said, "I hope you saw the humor in my message. Ha! Mr. Speedy Resume Service! Did you call the number?"

"No, I've had more important concerns." I didn't have a poker-face, but I put on something close to it.

## CHAPTER 34

"Now, Greg, you have to learn to laugh." Fred stood and began to pace the room. "Life is too short to waste in some sour mood."

"I'm fine, Fred. In fact, I feel the joy of the Lord in this place, so don't concern yourself about my mood."

"You can't be serious!" Fred scoffed. He wrapped his arms around himself like he had a chill. "This room gives me the creeps. Let's go to your study."

"I can't."

"What?!" Fred was impatient.

"We have guests—friends from San Diego. They pastor one of our churches down there. They'll be here any minute."

"Oh. Well, I guess I could. . . ." Fred trailed off. He lost his thought. "You know this room is distracting! What do we use it for?" He spun around and searched the walls.

"Prayer and ministry. You know, preservice prayer and ministry to folks who respond to the invitation."

"Oh, right, of course."

"What's on your mind, Fred? My resume or my resignation?"

"Now, you said that, not me," Fred shook his finger at me. "Still, I can't pretend that this isn't serious. I don't know how much longer I can keep the peace around here. There are a lot of folks very upset with you. We no sooner get rid of what's-his-name and his foolishness about prophets and spooky gifts, and then you start up with the same thing."

"Who? Who is upset?"

"Good grief, Greg! You should have been a lawyer! I can't break confidence." Fred sat down, leaned toward me, and lowered his voice. "Now, here's the thing, Greg. Maybe we can find a compromise. Try this on for size. What if you just stopped praying for folks—you know, the way you do? I think that would go a long way to making peace around here."

"You know what Jesus said?" I asked. "He said, 'Do not suppose that I have come to bring peace to the earth. I did not come to bring peace, but a sword.'"

"Cotton pick, Greg!" Fred stood and stamped his foot. "I swear, I don't know if you're stubborn or some kinda stupid. But you better come to your senses, or they are gonna vote your butt right out of that pulpit."

"Fred, do what you have to do. And I'll do what I have to do."

"Greg, I've considered you a friend—a good friend. You gave us ten good years."

"I've been here eleven."

"I know that. In those years, some people might say that your pastoral ability was a few donuts short of a dozen. You didn't always ring the bell. You couldn't—it wasn't in you. I understood that. But my friendship—well, the fondness we all had for you—covered those faults. We loved you anyway. But—" Fred paused and pawed the carpet with his toe. "But, gosh-darn-it, that fondness has run awful thin. We can't cover up what we see—not anymore."

There was a long silence.

"Don't you have anything to say for yourself?" Fred searched my face, but I stood silent. "Listen, Greg. I gotta get out of here before I grow hives. This room gives me jitters."

# Chapter 35

Fred exited through the door that led outside. I was glad for that because Tyler and BJ were in the sanctuary. I could hear the giggles.

"Hey, guys! What's all the racket out here?"

BJ was on the platform adjacent to the prayer room. She spun around and bubbled like a little girl pretending to be a ballerina.

"Oh, Greg," she gushed, "I feel the Lord's presence in this place."

I looked around the sanctuary. My eyes caught on the areas where others saw Deception and Pride. I was not as enthusiastic.

BJ saw me scan the pews. "I don't mean there, silly. Here! Right here on the platform." She had her hands out just as Sandy had. "Can you feel it?" She moved closer to me and to the wall shared by the prayer room.

I joined her. "Oh, my! Tyler, Martha come up here!" I called and motioned. "Do you feel anything?"

Martha remained seated in the front row. Tyler came up and put a hand on the wall. He extended his other hand toward the pulpit. "Greg, there's a river, a flow of God's presence from that room to your pulpit."

"What is that room?" BJ asked.

"Our prayer room. We prayed there yesterday for a man—a glorious deliverance. He came in bound by darkness. He believed that he would not see his next birthday. But he left quoting Scripture, passages he had never learned. This morning, he came by to say thanks, and he brought me an invitation to his birthday party. God's glory lingers in that room still today."

"No, Greg," Tyler said. "God's glory isn't fading. His anointing is *beginning* to flow. Your obedience and your willing spirit has brought God nearer. It's a promise and a blessing: *Draw near to God, and he will draw near to you.* It's like the baptism of Jesus. John saw the Spirit's presence. Jesus heard the Father's blessing. The Lord is pleased with you, Greg. He has gifts for you."

"He also has plans for you," BJ chimed in. "Tyler is right. We knew some of this before we came. It's why were here. God put you on our hearts weeks ago. We've been praying for you."

BJ left the platform and sat beside Martha. She placed a hand on her shoulder and said, "I've prayed lots for you, hon."

Martha answered with tears and choked on the emotion. When she found her voice, she said, "I'm just afraid."

"I know. The Lord showed me a vision of you in my prayer time. A storm was right over your house. Lightening and thunder rattled the windows and walls. You were under the bed. You prayed for the storm to pass."

"It's not as easy for me," Martha confessed. "Greg takes it all in stride. I take it all *inside*." She pointed to her chest.

BJ put an arm around Martha and said, "The Lord gave me a word for you. He says, 'I know you fear the storms. The thunders make you hide. But the storms are servants to accomplish my purpose. Judgment to one, refreshment to another. You have been marked for blessing. No harm will come to you. The winds will blow. But, like seed, they will blow you both into the fields that I have chosen.'"

Tyler added, "We want you both to know that we feel called to support you in prayer and intercession. Also, the Lord will give us words for you. I know that He will. Like here today. We hope that you will be open and receive what God gives us."

"You've changed, Tyler," I said to my friend. "I know you didn't get this in seminary. How does an American Baptist preacher like yourself get involved in things like this?"

"Well, I found out that God had postgraduate training available."

"Really? Where?"

"It's call the School of Spirit," Tyler answered. "And it takes place in any willing and humble heart. But the tuition is steep—too much for most." Tyler paused and looked me squarely in the eye. "It will cost you everything."

BJ hugged Martha closer and added, "But it gives you back much more."

"Why doesn't that comfort me?" Martha asked.

# Chapter 36

"Who called?" Martha asked.

"Oh, it was Russ," I answered. "You know, the executive minister."

"Don't tell me they got him involved."

"It seems that Harold and Fred presented a petition to the regional office. It was signed by a sufficient number of members." I had to sit down to process it all. Martha joined me on the sofa.

"How did it read?"

"Oh, well, the text was innocent enough. It just asked the regional officials to come have a look-see and mediate our little misunderstanding—according to Russ."

"So, what's next?"

"Well, we get a week off," I answered.

"Is that good?"

"Russ said we could use his cabin at Lake Arrowhead. He's gonna preach on Sunday. Then he'll meet with the board afterward."

"Are you worried?" Martha asked.

"No. The Lord is my defense. Jesus is my example, too. In 1 Peter it says, '*When they hurled their insults at him, he did not *retaliate; when he suffered, he made no threats. Instead, he entrusted himself to him who judges justly.'*

"Any problem the board—and whoever else—has with me doesn't deserve defending. And any problem they have with God doesn't need it. Jesus trusted the Father to defend him, and I'll do the same."

"Yeah, but they crucified Him!"

"I thought about that, too. I realized that the greatest place of surrender is the Cross. I can't control things from there. All I can do is trust."

# Chapter 37

I SIGNED THE CLIPBOARD, smiled at the receptionist, and found a seat. The waiting room was empty except for an old man with snow-white hair. I smiled and greeted him, "Good morning." I should have kept my mouth shut. The old-timer stood to his feet and took the chair next me.

"I see you're a God-fearin' man," he said.

"Oh, you mean because of the Bible?" I asked, and he nodded. "Well, I'm glad the waiting room has these Gideon Bibles. I rushed off without my quiet time this morning."

"Are ya sick?" the old-timer asked. He leaned over to get a close look at me.

"No. I just got a headache that won't go away." I pointed to the top of my head and said, "It's right here. I've never had one there before."

"You been buttin' your head into things lately?" he asked.

"What?"

"Oh, nothin'," the old-timer answered. "So how do ya figure it came on to ya? The headache, that is?"

## CHAPTER 37

"This last Sunday I had the day off. My wife and I visited the Anaheim Vineyard. I wanted to hear John Wimber. Anyway, right at the end, he prayed. That's when the headache hit me."

"Oh-oh," the old-timer grunted.

"We had the rest of the week off. We stayed in a friend's cabin. I was miserable all week. I figured I'd better get the doc to check it out."

"Check what out?" he asked.

"The headache, of course!" I spoke louder in case he was hard of hearing.

"Right, but I want to know what the pastor prayed for?"

"Oh, it was something to do with his sermon. He taught about how God equips His people to do the ministry He calls them to. He said something about how a duck has webbed feet, and that's a pretty good sign that he's called to water."

"What's he called you to? What's your equipment?"

*None of your business!* That's what I wanted to say. Instead, I answered, "First, I thought I was called to teach. I taught school for a while. Later on, I felt called to pastor. I do that now—at First Baptist. But I'm not sure where I belong anymore."

"Maybe that's why you're buttin' your head."

"What?!" I wondered if this guy was for real.

He continued, "You said you're not sure if you belong. So, maybe you're buttin' your head to get out. That's okay. I bet you're goin' to a better place."

"I already told you that I didn't butt my head up against anything."

"I know, I know," he said. "Let me ask you something. Have you ever seen a baby right after he's born?"

"Yeah, I saw my own."

"Some babies have a harder time, don't they? It's a real struggle to get out."

"I know." I was flooded with memories. "You should have seen my daughter. My wife was in labor for the whole day. The doc said the baby's head was too big. He almost had to do a C-section. She finally made it, but she looked like an alien. She had a cone head from all of the forces of the birth. Ouch! Her head was normal in a week or so, but, whew! What an ordeal!"

"Mr. Johnson," the receptionist called and motioned for me. "Have you filled out this form before?"

"I don't think so." I filled in the few blanks and signed the form. I returned to my seat.

The old-timer was gone, but the Bible lay open on my chair. The passage before me was from Galatians. My eyes found Paul's words, *"My dear children, for whom I am again in the pains of childbirth until Christ is formed in you. . . ."*

# Chapter 38

THE DOCTOR FOUND NOTHING WRONG WITH ME. He said that the next step was a long list of expensive tests, but he advised against it. "I've got a hunch, Greg," Dr. Snyder said, "that when you're past this trouble at church, your head will be okay."

"But what should I do in the meantime?" I asked.

"Well, if you had hurt a knee or an ankle, I'd say to stay off it for a while. I guess the same advice is good here. Stop using your head so much. Give it a rest."

I went home, but I felt no better. Martha asked, "Did Dr. Snyder give you pills?"

"No. He gave me a puzzle."

"You mean instead of the crayons or balloon?" Martha jested.

"You're not helping," I answered.

"Well, maybe you wiggled too much when he tried to get your temperature and blood pressure."

"His treatment advice was for me to stay off my head for a while. How do you figure?"

"Now, there's a wise doc!" Martha gloated.

## CHAPTER 38

"How am I supposed to do that?"

"This message from BJ might help." Martha lifted a note pad with her handwriting.

"What did she say?"

"In her prayer time for you, she received a message from the Lord. Are you okay with that?"

"Of course! What is it?"

"Well, she wanted me to ask. She also wants to know if you bear witness to this and if it makes sense to you." Martha returned to the notes. "She said the Lord is giving you an anointing one hundred times greater than before. You will have the gift of discernment. A new ministry is being born in and through you. But for God to birth this work, you must let go of your need to reason and think and figure everything out. God will give you new eyes to see His path, to see the enemy, to see the salvation of God." Martha put down the notes and asked, "So, does it make sense?"

"I think I get it. If I can get the swelling down in my head, then maybe this baby can be born."

"Maybe your other message—this one from Russ—will help the swelling."

"What did he say?"

"He complimented you for your fine board and staff. And then he asked that you call him to discuss some concerns he has. He sounded grave. In jest, I said, 'Well, should I pack our bags?' He didn't lighten up. Like a mortician, he said, 'Don't be concerned, Martha. I won't let them put you on the streets.'"

# Chapter 39

"Greg, I want to help you, but you've got to help yourself. How do you answer all of these charges?"

"Russ, I'm not going to defend myself or Scripture. It has taken me a few years to grow to this place of understanding. I can't explain it over the phone in a few minutes. My sermons are on tape. Our prayer sessions are recorded in journals. I have books in my library that might help you—"

"I'm not the one in need of help here, Greg," Russ interrupted.

"I know that. I just meant—"

"I know all of the arguments," Russ interrupted again. His patience was spent. "I teach the current issues class in the New Testament, remember? This isn't about theology; this is about church politics. All of those debates are fine, but they belong in the classroom. Here in the trenches it's about boards, budgets, buildings, and balance. You have to go along to get along."

"I used to think that, too, but I've changed, Russ. Programs don't matter; people do. God wants to release burdens, not raise budgets. He wants Spirit-led pastors who are hungry for God, not straight-laced politicians who are afraid to rock the boat."

"I see," Russ answered. Then silence.

"Well, what's next?" I wondered aloud. I heard a sigh and several deep breaths from Russ. "Well?" I prodded.

"The board has already called for a special business meeting. They asked me to officiate."

"What's the agenda, the stated purpose of the meeting?"

"It will be a vote of confidence on the pastor. There are some strong voices that believe you are unfit to lead the church, Greg." More silence. Russ wanted my response. I had none. He concluded the call and said, "I'm sorry, Greg. The notice will be mailed today."

# Chapter 40

"Before this meeting is over, I want to say a few words about Pastor Greg and his ministry. From my count, it seems like an even split—half of you don't like the changes around here and you doubt Pastor Greg's leadership. I'm with the other half. Some of us trust the man and believe he hears from God. Others of us have been a part of the changes and like the direction. Still others of us just want peace; it hurts 'em to see the church divided. But then there's some of us who have seen miracles. You've heard our stories. I don't know how anybody could discount that. Anyway, maybe my two cents worth won't matter. Still, I gotta say it.

"Most of you know that I'm a police officer. I've learned to be cautious and skeptical. I think that comes with the job. But I've had more than skepticism to overcome before God could get a hold of me. The enemy of my soul had stongholds in my life. He wanted to destroy my marriage, my family, my career—my very life. My wife had asked me to leave. She said she loved me, but she couldn't live with my violence and my unfaithfulness.

## CHAPTER 40

"I didn't know how to change. I was hopeless. I went to another woman's house for comfort, to spend the night. I was gonna get drunk so I couldn't feel the pain. But as soon as I got there, my pager went off. It was my daughter, my baby. I called home, and she answered. She just said, 'Daddy, I love you. Please come home.' It broke my heart. I wanted to go, but I knew I wasn't welcome.

"I left that woman's house in a rage. I wanted to kill the one person who had caused me all this pain. So, I drove to a lonely place and put one hollow-point bullet in my gun. The gun was in my lap for a long time. I felt sorry for myself, and the courage didn't come right away. Plus a hundred voices filled my head. Some said, 'Do it!' Others cried, 'Wait!' Then one final voice cut through the others. It was the only one that made sense. It said, 'Your wife said she loves you. She just can't live with the violence and unfaithfulness. You can't live with them, either. So why not ask God to take them away? Then you can go home—alone.'

"I needed help. I dug out Pastor Greg's business card and called him. I explained everything, and he said, 'Let's pray.' We prayed at the church. A few of you folks were there. What happened next still frightens me. My eyes were opened. I saw how every wrong choice in my life empowered demonic strongholds. I had lost control of my life.

"Forces that I still don't understand had come into my life from generations past. And these same evil powers were already at work in my children—because of me. Pastor prayed for me, but I had to choose Christ. Pastor counseled me, but I had to repent and make amends. Jesus healed and covered me, but I had to go back to my family and become a righteous covering for them."

He pointed to me, and his voice trembled. "God has used this man to work miracles in many lives. I'm his best agent. I bring half-a-dozen folks over every week, some in handcuffs!

"I just can't believe the foolishness I've heard in these meetings. I can't believe that someone would spread rumors as silly as these tales. Pastor never sprinkled salt on me, but he spoke God's Word to me. He never made me wear garlic, but he made me want God. He played no mind games, but he helped me find the mind of Christ.

"This man has been a gift from God to me. Some of you don't see that he's your gift, too. Be careful! If you don't appreciate the gift of God, He will give it to someone else who does. Ooops!" The speaker was startled by his pager. He reached to read the number. "It's my baby. She wants to know where daddy is. I told her that I'd bring home a treat. I will, but that's the *only* thing I'll bring home. Thank you, Pastor Greg."

# Epilogue

Jesus delivered and healed the man who lived among the tombs in Gad. The legion of demons was sent into pigs and drowned in the sea. The man who was beyond help was helped. Yet the people saw no miracle; they saw a menace. Jesus, the Son of God, was not worshiped; He was asked to leave.

In my case, the invitation to leave was a painful labor, but the result was a new birth of ministry in and through our lives. God has taken us to nations around the globe. He has fulfilled His word and kept His promises.

I know that God's desire is to set the captive free. He will use any willing vessel to carry the message. And He will show his deliverance to anyone who is willing to believe.

# APPENDIX I

# Related Scripture

## Ephesians 6:10–19

10 *Finally, be strong in the Lord and in his mighty power.*
11 *Put on the full armor of God so that you can take your stand against the devil's schemes.*
12 *For our struggle is not against flesh and blood, but against the rulers, against the authorities, against the powers of this dark world and against the spiritual forces of evil in the heavenly realms.*
13 *Therefore put on the full armor of God, so that when the day of evil comes, you may be able to stand your ground, and after you have done everything, to stand.*
14 *Stand firm then, with the belt of truth buckled around your waist, with the breastplate of righteousness in place,*
15 *and with your feet fitted with the readiness that comes from the gospel of peace.*
16 *In addition to all this, take up the shield of faith, with which you can extinguish all the flaming arrows of the evil one.*
17 *Take the helmet of salvation and the sword of the Spirit, which is the word of God.*
18 *And pray in the Spirit on all occasions with all kinds of prayers and requests. With this in mind, be alert and always keep on praying for all the saints.*
19 *Pray also for me, that whenever I open my mouth, words may be given me so that I will fearlessly make known the mystery of the gospel,*

## Mark 5:1–20

1  They went across the lake to the region of the Gerasenes.
2  When Jesus got out of the boat, a man with an evil spirit came from the tombs to meet him.
3  This man lived in the tombs, and no one could bind him any more, not even with a chain.
4  For he had often been chained hand and foot, but he tore the chains apart and broke the irons on his feet. No one was strong enough to subdue him.
5  Night and day among the tombs and in the hills he would cry out and cut himself with stones.
6  When he saw Jesus from a distance, he ran and fell on his knees in front of him.
7  He shouted at the top of his voice, "What do you want with me, Jesus, Son of the Most High God? Swear to God that you won't torture me!"
8  For Jesus had said to him, "Come out of this man, you evil spirit!"
9  Then Jesus asked him, "What is your name?" "My name is Legion," he replied, "for we are many."
10  And he begged Jesus again and again not to send them out of the area.
11  A large herd of pigs was feeding on the nearby hillside.
12  The demons begged Jesus, "Send us among the pigs; allow us to go into them."
13  He gave them permission, and the evil spirits came out and went into the pigs. The herd, about two thousand in number, rushed down the steep bank into the lake and were drowned.
14  Those tending the pigs ran off and reported this in the town and countryside, and the people went out to see what had happened.
15  When they came to Jesus, they saw the man who had been possessed by the legion of demons, sitting there, dressed and in his right mind; and they were afraid.
16  Those who had seen it told the people what had happened to the demon-possessed man—and told about the pigs as well.
17  Then the people began to plead with Jesus to leave their region.
18  As Jesus was getting into the boat, the man who had been demon-possessed begged to go with him.
19  Jesus did not let him, but said, "Go home to your family and tell them how much the Lord has done for you, and how he has had mercy on you."
20  So the man went away and began to tell in the Decapolis how much Jesus had done for him. And all the people were amazed.

## 1 Corinthians 2:1–5

1  When I came to you, brothers, I did not come with eloquence or superior wisdom as I proclaimed to you the testimony about God.
2  For I resolved to know nothing while I was with you except Jesus Christ and him crucified.
3  I came to you in weakness and fear, and with much trembling.
4  My message and my preaching were not with wise and persuasive words, but with a demonstration of the Spirit's power,
5  so that your faith might not rest on men's wisdom, but on God's power.

## Acts 10:36–40

36  You know the message God sent to the people of Israel, telling the good news of peace through Jesus Christ, who is Lord of all.
37  You know what has happened throughout Judea, beginning in Galilee after the baptism that John preached—
38  how God anointed Jesus of Nazareth with the Holy Spirit and power, and how he went around doing good and healing all who were under the power of the devil, because God was with him.
39  "We are witnesses of everything he did in the country of the Jews and in Jerusalem. They killed him by hanging him on a tree,
40  but God raised him from the dead on the third day and caused him to be seen.

## Romans 6:11–16

11  In the same way, count yourselves dead to sin but alive to God in Christ Jesus.
12  Therefore do not let sin reign in your mortal body so that you obey its evil desires.
13  Do not offer the parts of your body to sin, as instruments of wickedness, but rather offer yourselves to God, as those who have been brought from death to life; and offer the parts of your body to him as instruments of righteousness.
14  For sin shall not be your master, because you are not under law, but under grace.
15  What then? Shall we sin because we are not under law but under grace? By no means!
16  Don't you know that when you offer yourselves to someone to obey him as slaves, you are slaves to the one whom you obey—whether you are slaves to sin, which leads to death, or to obedience, which leads to righteousness?

## 1 Corinthians 12:1–31

1. Now about spiritual gifts, brothers, I do not want you to be ignorant.
2. You know that when you were pagans, somehow or other you were influenced and led astray to mute idols.
3. Therefore I tell you that no one who is speaking by the Spirit of God says, "Jesus be cursed," and no one can say, "Jesus is Lord," except by the Holy Spirit.
4. There are different kinds of gifts, but the same Spirit.
5. There are different kinds of service, but the same Lord.
6. There are different kinds of working, but the same God works all of them in all men.
7. Now to each one the manifestation of the Spirit is given for the common good.
8. To one there is given through the Spirit the message of wisdom, to another the message of knowledge by means of the same Spirit,
9. to another faith by the same Spirit, to another gifts of healing by that one Spirit,
10. to another miraculous powers, to another prophecy, to another distinguishing between spirits, to another speaking in different kinds of tongues, and to still another the interpretation of tongues.
11. All these are the work of one and the same Spirit, and he gives them to each one, just as he determines.
12. The body is a unit, though it is made up of many parts; and though all its parts are many, they form one body. So it is with Christ.
13. For we were all baptized by one Spirit into one body—whether Jews or Greeks, slave or free—and we were all given the one Spirit to drink.
14. Now the body is not made up of one part but of many.
15. If the foot should say, "Because I am not a hand, I do not belong to the body," it would not for that reason cease to be part of the body.
16. And if the ear should say, "Because I am not an eye, I do not belong to the body," it would not for that reason cease to be part of the body.
17. If the whole body were an eye, where would the sense of hearing be? If the whole body were an ear, where would the sense of smell be?
18. But in fact God has arranged the parts in the body, every one of them, just as he wanted them to be.
19. If they were all one part, where would the body be?
20. As it is, there are many parts, but one body.
21. The eye cannot say to the hand, "I don't need you!" And the head cannot say to the feet, "I don't need you!"

22 On the contrary, those parts of the body that seem to be weaker are indispensable,
23 and the parts that we think are less honorable we treat with special honor. And the parts that are unpresentable are treated with special modesty,
24 while our presentable parts need no special treatment. But God has combined the members of the body and has given greater honor to the parts that lacked it,
25 so that there should be no division in the body, but that its parts should have equal concern for each other.
26 If one part suffers, every part suffers with it; if one part is honored, every part rejoices with it.
27 Now you are the body of Christ, and each one of you is a part of it.
28 And in the church God has appointed first of all apostles, second prophets, third teachers, then workers of miracles, also those having gifts of healing, those able to help others, those with gifts of administration, and those speaking in different kinds of tongues.
29 Are all apostles? Are all prophets? Are all teachers? Do all work miracles?
30 Do all have gifts of healing? Do all speak in tongues? Do all interpret?
31 But eagerly desire the greater gifts. And now I will show you the most excellent way.

## APPENDIX II

# Related Terms

**Gift of Discernment**

*The gift of discernment is a spiritual gift given to believers, according to 1 Corinthians 12:10. The gift is described as "distinguishing of spirits" in the NAS, "distinguishing between spirits" in the NIV, and "discerning of spirits" in the NKJV.*

The key to understanding the gift of discernment is accurately defining *diakrisis*, the Greek word rendered "discernment." The word means "to make a judgment on the basis of careful and detailed information, to judge carefully, to evaluate carefully." The word is used in three different passages in the New Testament: 1 Corinthians 12:10 (above), Romans 14:1, and Hebrews 5:14. I believe that Hebrews 5:14 is the key in understanding the biblical concept of discernment. The verse is translated in the New American Standard Bible as "But solid food is for the mature, who because of practice have their senses trained to discern good and evil." The word *senses* is aistheterion and is defined as "sensory perception." The noun is translated "sense," or "organ of sense."[1]

The verse would seem to indicate that the one who is mature has so exercised his senses that he is a mature believer who can discern good and evil.

The emphasis of the word is on the result of the discernment, not on the method. The English word *discern* is defined by Webster's Dictionary as (1) to detect with the eyes, and (2) to detect with senses other than vision. The Greek word would enlarge this definition to include any way of knowing spiritual realities. The other revelatory gifts—words of knowledge, words of wisdom, prophetic words, visions, and dreams—appear to be released primarily through the mind, rather than the senses.

How, then, does spiritual discernment work? This discernment operates primarily through the physical (and Spiritual) senses and the mind and is used to evaluate whether something is of God or of Satan. Peter Wagner defines the gift of discernment as "the special ability that God gives to some members of the Body of Christ to know with assurance whether certain behavior purported to be of God is in reality divine, human or satanic,"[2] as well as the ability to detect a Christian's motives, whether godly or carnal and the supernatural ability to distinguish truth from error, regardless of motive. He believes this gift is given to relatively few people and might not be exercised frequently.

During the course of the last several years, I have found that I have, through my five senses, discerned many spiritual realities. One of the first experiences I had was with my wife in a worship service. Together, we both felt the brush of angel's wings. I have since had a physical reaction to the presence of demons, angels, witchcraft, spiritual powers, and authorities. (According to Ephesians 6:12, which refers to "rulers, authorities, powers and spiritual forces of evil," there are hierarchies among both fallen angels and godly angels.) I have been able to tell with my hands whether certain objects are demonic or righteous. I have on a couple of occasions smelled a sulfur-like substance and rotting garbage where no physical garbage was present, and I associate that with evil. I have been physically aware of angels bringing messages. Recently, I have on several occasions seen a light out of the corner of my eye, gone over to where the light was, and realized through a physical sensation that I had seen the flash of an angel. Other people, present with me, have confirmed that they also sense what I have discerned. Although I have not heard any spiritual sounds, I have worked with those who have heard the Lord speak audibly, angels sing, demons talk and laugh, and horses' hooves thunder by. Others have been able to identify righteous and unrighteous spiritual beings by a kind of internal "knowing." My wife Donna, for example, often knows that a demonic power is present even though she has no sensory reaction.

**Prophecy**
> *"The gift of prophecy is the special ability that God gives to certain members of the Body of Christ to receive and communicate an immediate message of God to His people through a divinely anointed utterance."*[3]

During the prayer session, the Lord will use this gift to reveal actual memories of the person being prayed for. One may see pictures of the actual events in the generation past. (Note: I believe that when people have reincarnation experiences, they are actually seeing the demonic right to the bondage the person is currently experiencing.) One may also get names of demonic strongholds. As the Lord reveals information, one can ask questions of the Lord. Remember that this is a conversation.

For one week we had the privilege of ministering to three generations—parents, children, and grandchildren—who were living on one piece of property in Colorado. The parents had been missionaries in New Guinea and this was where the children had experienced their childhood. One of their sons had been unfaithful to his wife and was constantly fighting against lust and pornography. The marriage was at a crisis point. As the prayer team ministered, one intercessor had a clear vision of a three-year-old kid being taken into the jungle. She told me privately what she had seen, but I felt that we should not reveal anything without further confirmation from the Lord.

As we entered into the next prayer time, the man still had no relevant memories of his childhood. As I looked at his wife, I felt prompted to tell her that I sensed that she would see what had happened to her husband. She began to have a vision of three-year-old boys being taken into the jungle by local natives. I asked what happened next, and she said that these natives performed an idolatrous ritual over them and then sodomized them. That event had opened an unrelenting demonic attack against her husband, opening all types of sexual attacks against him. In prayer we broke the power of the demon, and the man began to walk in new freedom.

Dreams are apparently a category of the gift of prophecy that the Lord often uses in a prayer session. At times, the Lord will give me a dream before a prayer session for understanding as to the approach I am to take in ministry. While ministering in Colorado, I had a four-part dream. The next day, while I was ministering to a woman, the Lord brought the dream back to my memory. I recalled each step and then in prayer the team discerned what we were to do. We followed each of those steps, and the woman began to move in greater freedom.

While we were ministering in Toronto, our two-year-old granddaughter, who lives with her parents in southern California, began to cry uncontrollably. At times she would scream continually for more than two hours. This went on for more than three days. I would call on the phone, pray for her, and the crying would stop briefly. Finally, after eliciting the help of several intercessors, the screaming stopped. I asked the Lord why she was under such attack, and I had a dream of a black bird the size of a horse, attacking me from the air. As I pondered the dream, I remembered that my wife often had a recurring dream into adulthood of black birds attacking her. When we returned home we prayed with my wife and discovered that some hundred plus generations back the Celtic people in her line had been involved with curses revolving around black birds. We canceled these curses over her and over our children and grandchildren, and the screaming has no longer been an issue. The terror that our granddaughter had been experiencing disappeared.

## Word of Knowledge

> "The gift of knowledge is the special ability that God gives to certain members of the Body of Christ to discover, accumulate, analyze, and clarify information and ideas that are pertinent to the growth and well-being of the Body of Christ—and of it's individual members."[4]

During the prayer session, there are times when biblical knowledge, spiritual principles, and personal information is given to the individuals who are praying or being prayed for. The purpose of the word of knowledge is to help aid the Body of Christ in their spiritual growth.

## Tongues

> "The gift of tongues is the special ability that God gives to certain members of the Body of Christ to accomplish one of the following: 1) to speak to God in language they have never learned, and 2) to receive and communicate an immediate message of God to His people through a divinely anointed utterance in a language they have never learned."[5]

Often, this gift is used either to open up the heavens so that truth about the person's life and generations may be revealed or to increase the strength of the warfare.

## Interpretation of Tongues

> *"The gift of interpretation of tongues is the special ability that God gives to certain members of the Body of Christ to make known, in the vernacular, the message of one who speaks in tongues."*[6]

As the gift of tongues is exercised, the interpretation brings understanding to what the Lord is doing and saying in the prayer session. I might add that one must be sensitive to the context in which these gifts are exercised. If someone has difficulty accepting these gifts, then one must be sensitive to them and only exercise the gift quietly.

## Healing

> *"The gift of healing is the special ability that God gives to certain members of the Body of Christ to serve as human intermediaries through whom it pleases God to cure illness and restore health apart from the use of natural means."*[7]

Many, but not all, illnesses have a demonic root. Jesus at times healed with a focus on the physical disease; at other times, Jesus healed by casting out the demon (Matt 4:24). After a deliverance, the Lord at times leads us to pray for the physical healing of an individual.

## Mercy

> "The gift of mercy is the special ability that God gives to certain members of the Body of Christ to feel genuine empathy and compassion for individuals, both Christian and non-Christian, who suffer distressing physical, mental, or emotional problems and to translate that compassion into cheerfully done deeds that reflect Christ's love and alleviate the suffering."[8]

This gift is a very powerful in a prayer session. At times, we find that those who have this gift begin to weep uncontrollably. This weeping has a very powerful affect on the person being prayed for. They understand that the Lord really does comprehend the depth of their sorrow and pain. We have learned, however, that discernment must be used in the exercise of this gift. At times, it is necessary for the person being prayed for to experience the totality of their emotions, without any physical expression of love being expressed.

## Deliverance

> "The gift of deliverance is the special ability that God gives to certain members of the Body of Christ to cast out demons and evil spirits."[9]

It is very helpful, if not essential, for the leader of the prayer session to be gifted with the gift of deliverance. Through his guidance and God-given authority, he directs the prayer session.

## Intercession

> *"The gift of intercession is the special ability that God gives to certain members of the Body of Christ to pray for extended periods of time on a regular basis and see frequent and specific answers to their prayers to a degree much greater than that which is expected of the average Christian."*

This gift seems to be exercised mainly in private. It is in the prayer closet that the foundational work of the ministry of deliverance is laid. In the prayer session, the silent prayers of individuals present are essential to all of the ministry taking place. Simply because an intercessor might not receive information does not negate the key role that that person plays in the deliverance. They are an equally important part of the prayer time.

## Teaching

> *"The gift of teaching is the special ability that God gives to certain members of the Body of Christ to communicate information relevant to the health and ministry of the Body and its members such that others will learn."* [10]

This gift, used with the gift of knowledge and wisdom, may be used in the session to bring to the forefront biblical truth relevant to the ministry at hand.

## Wisdom

> *"The gift of wisdom is the special ability that God gives to certain members of the Body of Christ to know the mind of the Holy Spirit such as to receive insight into how given knowledge may best be applied to specific needs arising in the Body of Christ."*[11]

Often, as the demon leaves, a person can feel a void in their mind. They can be confused and wonder who they are. At this point, those people who have the gift of wisdom can begin to fill the person's mind with the wisdom of God and can gently share biblical insights that are essential to the maturing of the newly freed believer.

## Faith

> *"The gift of faith is the special ability that God gives to some members of the Body of Christ to discern with extraordinary confidence the will and purposes of God for the future of His work."*[12]

I believe that faith is often linked with other gifts. I noticed that after the initial deliverance that I led, I would come to each deliverance session unequivocally believing that the Lord would come in power to set a person free. I noticed that those who have the gift of physical healing, when praying for physical healing for others, also come with an unnatural confidence that the Lord will work in power. I also knew that I did not have that confidence. It was not that I did not believe that God could heal; rather, I did not have a conviction of certainty that I would experience in a deliverance session. I realized that this faith in a deliverance session was a gift from the Lord.

## Exhortation

*"The gift of exhortation is the special ability that God gives to certain members of the Body of Christ to minister words of comfort, consolation, encouragement, and counsel to other members of the Body such that they feel helped and healed."* [13]

Many people who come for prayer are discouraged or at the point of hopelessness. They need comfort (the root word for *exhortation* in the Greek New Testament is *comfort*), encouragement, and a new direction in their lives. Exhortation is just what the doctor ordered, especially at the end of a prayer session. After the person has felt the devastation of the past and has seen some of the generational pollution that has seeped into the family line, one is ready for the comfort of the Lord and guidance for the future.

1. Gerhard Kittel and Friedrich Gerhard, eds. *The Theological Dictionary of the New Testament*, abridged in one volume. Grand Rapids: William B. Eerdmans Publishing Company, 1985.
2. C. Peter Wagner. *Your Spiritual Gifts Can Help Your Church Grow*. Ventura: Gospel Light, 1994, p. 96.
3. Wagner,. P. 200
4. Wagner. p. 190.
5. Wagner.p. 203.
6. Wagner. p. 206.
7. Wagner. p. 210.
8. Wagner, p. 194.
9. Wagner, p. 97.
10. Wagner, p. 119.
11. Wagner, p. 192.
12. Wagner, p. 146.
13. Wagner, p. 142.

APPENDIX III

# Lessons in Deliverance

**A Simple Model of Deliverance**

1. Ask at least two other believers to join you as part of the prayer team.
2. Use a prayer of renunciation. For example: *In the Name of Jesus Christ and by the Power of His blood I cancel any oaths, covenants, agreements, rituals, or spells made against me—with or without my will. I break pronouncements made against me. I break any ungodly soul ties.*
3. At this point, ask the Holy Spirit to come and rest on the person and to reveal any event in the past that allowed the enemy to come in. Deal with any issue that comes up (e.g., forgiveness or confession of sin). Ask the Lord to cover the memory with His blood. Ask the Lord how many generations back that demon was empowered. Ask the Lord to take the person back to that memory of the event (the demon often carries the memory of the event as the legal right to remain). Renounce and repent for the sins of that event (identification repentance) and ask

the Lord to break all ungodly connections between that event through the generation to the present and to that person's children to a thousand generations. As you count down, sense in each generation if other events took place. Ask the Lord to separate all human parts from Satan's creatures and demand that all evil go to the place that Jesus sends it.

## Generational Prayer For Deliverance (Outline)

1. Pray protection over yourself, family, and the person for whom you are praying.
2. Invite the Holy Spirit to come.
3. Ask the Lord to take the person back to any memory or recurring dream that He wants the person to deal with.
4. What is the issue the Lord wants to deal with? (fear, anger, lust, etc.)
5. How many generations back was this issue empowered in the family line?
6. In what country did this event take place?
7. What happened in that generation in the past?
8. Renunication and repentance for the issue (issues)
   "I renounce _____ in the name of Jesus Christ."
9. Have the person cancel any generational evil from the beginning of time to the discerned generation.
10. Begin counting down. Stop and deal with whatever issues the Lord brings up as you are counting down.
11. Be sensitive to and deal appropriately with any physical sensations, emotions, or visions.

12. Resume counting (by tens, fives, or ones) to the present, to children, to grandchildren, and to 1,000 generations.
13. Command all that evil to leave in the name of Jesus and to go to the place Jesus would send it.
14. Pray that the Lord restore any generational blessings, anointings, and giftings that may have been stolen.
15. Seal any entry points that the enemy may have opened, and seal the work that the Lord has done.

## Listening —the Key to Victory

I still have the same feeling as I sit down before an individual seeking prayer. Even though I have prayed for hundreds of individuals, I still often think to myself as I sit there, *I really have no hint of what to do.* So we sit there before the Lord and ask that the Holy Spirit would come and give us instruction. He has never yet failed! I am beginning to understand that I really can do nothing without Him (John 15:5; John 5:19).

## Prayer Team—the Key to Strength

Late in 1989, as I began doing deliverances, I realized that I was unable to understand what the Lord wanted to do during the prayer sessions. Of necessity, I would invite two to three others to join me as we prayed. I could begin the session and see manifestations of the demon, but I had no real understanding as to what the Lord was saying or what was happening spiritually. As others joined the prayer sessions, I was amazed at the giftedness of these individuals. Because we were concerned that we not be mislead by the enemy, we would use yellow tablets to write down all that the Lord was saying. I would ask questions of the enemy (the Lord has since instructed me not to do this!), and those who were present would hear answers and write them down. My yellow tablet usually remained unmarked.

We would operate under the principle that if we had two persons agreeing on the answer, we would take that as a confirmation. As we prayed, these people, whom I had pastored for several years, began to see and hear from the Lord. I was bewildered by what the Lord would continually show them. How could so many gifts be in the church and I still remain clueless?

As we learned to become a team, I became excited to see how the body of Christ could work together. Each person felt a sense of satisfaction as they were used of the Lord to help lead a person out of bondage. No person on the team was more important than another. Even those who sat and prayed and received nothing from the Lord realized that they had played an important part in the ministry. At last, I saw a real-life illustration of 1 Corinthians 12:7, *"Now to each one the manifestation of the Spirit is given for the common good."*

# APPENDIX IV

# Suggested Reading

Anderson, Neil. *The Bondage Breaker*. Eugene, Ore.: Harvest House, 1990.
Anderson, Neil. *Freedom In Christ*. Ventura, Calif.: Regal Books, 1995.
Arnold, Clinton E. *Three Crucial Questions about Spiritual Warfare*. Grand Rapids: Baker Books, 1997.
Boyd, Gregory. *God at War*. Chariot Family Publishing, 1994.
Fortune, Don and Katie. *Discover Your God-Given Gifts*. Grand Rapids: Chosen Books, 1999.
Gibson, Noel and Phyllis. *Evicting Demonic Intruders*. West Sussex, England: New Wine Press, 1993.
Greig, Gary S., and Kevin N. Springer, ed. *The Kingdom and the Power*. Ventura, Calif.: Regal Books, 1993.
Horrobin, Peter. *Healing Through Deliverance—The Biblical Basis*. Kent, England: Sovereign World, Ltd., 1995.
Horrobin, Peter. *Healing Through Deliverance—The Practical Ministry*. Kent, England: Sovereign World, Ltd., 1995.
Kraft, Charles. *Christianity With Power: Your Worldview and your Experience of the Supernatural*. Ann Arbor: Vine Books, 1989.
Kraft, Charles. *Deep Wounds, Deep Healing*. Ann Arbor, Mich.: Servant Publishing, 1993.
Kraft, Charles. *Defeating Dark Angels*. Ventura: Regal Books, 1990.
MacNutt, Francis. *Deliverance from Evil Spirits*. Grand Rapids, Michigan: Chosen Books, 1995.
Murphy, Fred. *The Handbook for Spiritual Warfare*. Nashville: Thomas Nelson Publishing, 1992.

Prince, Derek. *Blessing or Curse.* Grand Rapids : Chosen Books, 1993.

Prince, Derek. *They Shall Expel Demons.* Grand Rapids: Chosen Books, 1998.

Unger, Merrill. *What Demons Can Do to Christians.* Chicago: Moody Press, 1991.

Wagner, C. Peter. *Your Spiritual Gifts Can Help Your Church Grow.* Ventura: Regal, 1994.

Wagner, Doris M. *How To Cast Out Demons: A Beginner's Guide.* Ventura: Gospel Light, 1999.